Advanced Walleye Strategies

Advanced Walleye Strategies

Complete Angler's Library®
North American Fishing Club
Minneapolis, Minnesota

Advanced Walleye Strategies

Library of Congress Catalog Card Number 92-62042
ISBN 0-914697-52-8

Printed in U.S.A.
         3   4   5   6   7   8   9

The North American Fishing Club
offers a line of hats for fishermen.
For information, write:
        North American Fishing Club
        P.O. Box 3403
        Minnetonka, MN 55343

Contents

Acknowledgments

The North American Fishing Club would like to thank all those who helped create this book.

Wildlife artist Virgil Beck created the cover art. Artist David Rottinghaus provided all illustrations. Photos, in addition to the author's, were provided by Berkley, Paul DeMarchi, Complete Angler's Library Managing Editor Ron Larsen and *North American Fisherman* Editor Steve Pennaz.

A special thanks to the NAFC's publication staff for all their efforts: Publisher Mark LaBarbera, *North American Fisherman* Editor Steve Pennaz, Managing Editor of Books Ron Larsen, Associate Editor of Books Colleen Ferguson and Editorial Assistant of Books Victoria Brouillette. Thanks also to Vice President of Product Marketing Mike Vail, Marketing Manager Cal Franklin and Marketing Project Coordinator Laura Resnik.

About The Author

Walleye fishing isn't a matter of life and death, it's much more than that! Mark Romanack takes the subject of walleye fishing very seriously. An accomplished tournament professional, Romanack has cut his teeth on the Masters Walleye Club and Cabela's Professional Walleye Trail tournament circuits. An MWC top-50 qualifier, Mark has a never-ending desire for walleye fishing knowledge that helps to keep him at the top.

Mark's experience on the tournament trail is evident in his writing. Providing solid information on how, when and where to find walleyes and first-class, walleye-fishing action is definitely his specialty.

A graduate of Northern Michigan University, Mark holds a bachelor of science degree in fisheries and wildlife management. After working as an environmental educator for five years, he became a freelance outdoor writer in 1987.

As an outdoor communicator, Mark has had his articles and photographs appear in a number of top national and regional outdoor publications and fishing magazines, including NAFC's *North American Fisherman*. Mark estimates that he writes over 150 articles and takes hundreds of photographs each year.

Author of *Big Walleyes with Bob Propst*, Mark also is one of the authors for the NAFC's Complete Angler's Library book titled

Freshwater Fishing Secrets II and has collaborated on other books covering the subject of fishing. Action photos of walleyes and other gamefish have become his trademark.

In addition to his freelance work, Mark is an editor for a western Michigan outdoor newspaper. He also serves as a field editor for two Michigan outdoor magazines. Owner of his own outdoor consulting and photography business (Mark Romanack's Outdoor Communications) he has helped dozens of fishing and hunting manufacturers highlight their products.

An active member of the Outdoor Writers Association of America, Mark lives with his wife, Mari, and dog Buddy on the shores of Lake Mitchell in northern Michigan.

Dedication

Compiling, writing, editing and publishing a book is far from an individualistic effort. Many dedicated individuals have had an impact on the successful completion of this book.

To thank every person with whom I've shared walleye-fishing information is impossible, but a select group of individuals deserves special credit for their efforts.

As a tournament fisherman, I've crossed the boat wakes of our nation's most enterprising walleye anglers. Along the way, bits and pieces of fishing information passed hands and minds. It's these professional anglers who deserve much of the credit for developing and popularizing the walleye-fishing tactics writers so frequently pen, and anglers eventually take for granted.

Men such as Gary Parsons, Mike McClelland, Bob Propst, Gary Roach, Keith Kavajecz, Stan Berry, Mark Martin and many others have contributed greatly to my overall walleye-fishing knowledge and my development as a tournament angler. More than just good fishermen, these anglers have always been good friends and confidants.

As an outdoor writer, one person stands alone as my hero. The man who first noticed my talents, focused my ambition and encouraged me to take the outdoor writing business seriously is the man who later helped me negotiate my first major book contract.

Of all the gifts I've received in my life, David Richey, *Detroit News* outdoor writer, provided me with the most valuable gifts. Dave taught me how to make an outdoor story entertaining and educational. He showed me the difference between simply telling a story and marketing it. And most importantly, he proved to me that working harder than the other guy is the best way to become successful. Dave helped me make fishing and hunting my passion and lifelong ambition. In short, he guided me to a career in the outdoors.

Finally, no project of this magnitude would be complete without thanking my lovely wife, Mari, who supported me from day one and kept me going. Her business talents were invaluable when a computer glitch meant retyping chapter after chapter of text and laboring over a nightmare of software problems.

Together, I thank everyone for making this book project the best it could be and the North American Fishing Club for seeing the need for still another book on walleye fishing.

Foreword

Your hands hold a book that couldn't have been written 15, or even 10, years ago. Why? Because walleye-fishing knowledge has exploded in recent years. Need proof? Turn to the table of contents of this book. Yesterday's walleye anglers never heard of such tactics as "structure trolling cranks," "bottom bouncers," "power trolling" or, in many cases, "slip bobbering." Many of these techniques and tactics simply did not exist, or they were used only in very localized areas.

Things began changing in the mid-1980s when the Manufacturers Walleye Council (now the Masters Walleye Circuit), the nation's first walleye circuit, was formed. Its teams traveled to various walleye waters across North America, bringing a host of walleye-catching techniques. When the dust settled, we learned that many walleye-fishing "rules" were incorrect and walleyes were not as finicky as we thought. New techniques were developed and old techniques were refined and improved.

It was this evolution, make that explosion, of walleye-fishing knowledge that has made *Advanced Walleye Strategies* possible. It contains the latest walleye-fishing information—the information you need to become a consistently successful walleye angler. Author Mark Romanack, an MWC angler who has fished with and against the country's top walleye anglers, tapped into numerous outlets of walleye knowledge while writing this book. The result is a powerful source of information that was not available anywhere until now.

Advanced Walleye Strategies focuses on all aspects of walleye fishing: rigging the ultimate walleye boat, selecting the right tackle, finding fish when others can't and more. But the strength of this book is its focus on the hottest, yet often misunderstood, walleye-catching techniques ever developed. In these pages, you'll learn how to fish live-bait rigs more effectively, use bottom bouncers to their maximum effectiveness, utilize tips on slip bobbering and troll cranks for open-water suspended fish—the hottest bite in many waters.

Walleyes have long been the favorite fish for anglers across most of the northern states and Canada. That popularity has expanded virtually nationwide due, in part, to extensive stocking in a number of southern and western states.

This is extremely good news for thousands of NAFC anglers whose only choice in years past was to pack up and head for the traditional walleye haunts. Now those same anglers can almost literally find trophy-quality marble eyes in their own backyards. Romanack details the walleye spread across the country and reveals how to bring these fish into the boat.

So, not only do we know more about walleyes' habits and habitats, but there are more fish in more diverse waters to be chased and caught. Numerous fisheries biologists deserve a lot of credit for the tremendously popular stocking programs that have taken place outside the traditional walleye areas. Without their help, walleye-fishing opportunities would be much more limited. If you're a serious trophy fisherman, keep an eye on development of the walleye fisheries in these non-traditional areas for two reasons: (1) Walleyes grow fast in many of the Southern states where they are stocked; in fact, one of the oldest world records—the 25-pound walleye—came from Old Hickory Lake in Tennessee. (2) Few anglers know how to effectively fish walleyes in these new areas; hence, fishing pressure is low.

Walleyes can be among the easiest of fish to catch; they can also be the most difficult. That is why even professional anglers are excited when a successful pattern develops. Professional anglers spend a lot of time on the water. They document what works and what doesn't in order to reduce the amount of time spent trying to find walleyes. This book allows you to figuratively look over their shoulders in order to learn more about the science of walleye angling.

And that's exactly why we commissioned Mark to do this book. NAFC Members across the country have asked for more help in catching these fish; it was just a matter of putting together the kind of book that would be most helpful to the "serious" walleye angler.

Whether you are a beginner or expert, however, *Advanced Walleye Strategies* will help you catch more walleyes.

Steve Pennaz
Executive Director
North American Fishing Club

Getting To Know Walleyes

1

Walleyes Then And Now

Walleyes are fast becoming one of the nation's most prized gamefish. A major reason is that the fish are backed by an enthusiastic and growing army of admirers. Walleye fishing has come a long way, maturing more in the last 10 years than anyone could have predicted. The range of the sportfish whose popularity was limited to parts of Canada and the upper Midwest has grown to where the walleye (*Stizostedion vitreum vitreum*) is now available in catchable numbers in most of the lower 48 states and five Canadian provinces.

Obviously, there is better fishing in some regions than others; however, the fire to stock, manage and promote walleye fishing is spreading throughout the country. The fact that anglers nationwide are jumping on the walleye's bandwagon isn't difficult to understand.

It's tough not to like the walleye as a sportfish. Walleyes are a challenge to find and catch; they fight stubbornly on light tackle. In addition, few fish can compare with the walleye's delicate and delicious flavor when the meat is fried, baked or broiled.

Walleyes also are fast-growing fish that are easily raised in hatcheries. Stocking programs are a major reason why the species has expanded in range and exploded in population. In fact, stocking efforts within the last 10 years have improved a high percentage of the nation's best walleye-fishing waters. Fisheries managers around the country love to stock walleyes because the stocking is successful wherever the fish has abundant forage in the form of

Resource management teams across the country have been intensely implementing walleye stocking programs. Walleye fingerlings thrive and grow in waters with abundant forage.

Walleyes Then And Now

baitfish, ample room to grow and suitable water depth.

Walleyes thrive in large inland lakes, the Great Lakes, major rivers and reservoir systems; they are seldom found in small bodies of water. Fisheries with exceptionally deep and cold water for trout and salmon are not necessary for walleyes.

Biologists have determined from radio trackings that walleyes prefer a depth averaging 10 feet. However, the species is often found at greater depths and, at times, in water shallower than 10 feet. Still, these research findings provide anglers with some valuable clues as to where to start fishing for these prized gamefish.

Although often considered "fickle fish" that are difficult to catch, walleyes can be easily tempted into biting. When found in significant numbers, walleyes actually are no more (or less) difficult to catch than their close cousin, the yellow perch.

Major Task Is Finding Them

Finding concentrations of walleyes is the challenge. Walleye tournament professional Mike McClelland perhaps said it best: "Walleyes aren't tough to catch, they're hard to find." To some, McClelland's approach to walleye fishing may seem like an oversimplification, but to those who have spent countless hours in search of walleyes, Mike's words ring true on every outing.

Catching more walleyes depends less upon the rods, reels, line, lures and bait used than most anglers realize. All the latest tactics and equipment will not help if the lure isn't presented in close proximity to waiting walleyes.

Learning to accurately determine where these prized fish are likely to be found on any given day is the real secret to walleye fishing. Quite simply, anglers who can find fish will probably catch them, but, of course, it helps to have angling and presentation skills. Still, the most successful walleye fishing trips are built around finding and catching fish.

In the early days of modern walleye fishing, finding the fish was a major undertaking. Few anglers had depthfinders and most who had them knew little about using them effectively.

The development and marketing of sonar for the sport of fishing—specifically the flasher—provided the initiative for anglers to begin exploring the underwater world of the walleye. Prior to flashers, finding walleyes was like throwing darts at a target in the dark. Once in awhile an angler might hit the target, but consist-

Tournament professional Mike McClelland has been quoted many times saying, "Walleyes aren't tough to catch, they're just hard to find." Walleyes appeal to anglers of all skill levels.

Walleyes Then And Now 15

Structure fishing has had an impact on the popularity of walleye fishing. Dependable structure and depthfinders, such as flashers, made it possible during the '60s and early '70s for walleye anglers to explore the offshore regions of popular walleye fisheries for the first time.

ently hitting the bull's-eye was a rare occasion.

As the flasher grew in popularity as an angling tool, more and more fishermen found and caught walleyes on a regular basis. Then came the dawn of the structure-fishing era, and angling pioneers such as Al and Ron Lindner, Buck Perry, Bill Binkelman and others explored and shared the world of walleye fishing for almost two decades.

The early students of walleye fishing learned more about walleyes and how to catch them than anyone had ever dreamed possible. Classic fishing presentations such as Lindy Rigging, backtrolling and spoon plugging were born and filled the pages of outdoor magazines.

The popularity of walleye fishing spread throughout the walleye heartland. Lakes and rivers in Minnesota, Wisconsin, South Dakota, North Dakota, Nebraska and southern Ontario, Manitoba and Saskatchewan became meccas for walleye fishing. Gradually other states including Illinois, Michigan, Ohio and Iowa gained a share of the wealth of walleye fishing.

It wasn't until the first walleye tournaments appeared during the early 1970s that the sport of walleye fishing was transformed from a weekend pastime into a virtually full-time preoccupation among a cult-like collection of anglers hungry for fishing information. Following in the footsteps of major bass-fishing circuits, the first walleye-fishing tournament circuits were organized in Minnesota, Wisconsin, Nebraska and North and South Dakota.

Most leading walleye professionals of the late '80s and early '90s got their start in these early competitions. In fact, those competitions could have been considered their "training grounds." These tournament anglers developed many of the most successful walleye-fishing presentations:

- Slip-sinker rigging
- Bottom-bouncer tactics
- Slip-bobber basics
- Trolling for suspended walleyes with in-line planer boards
- Use of segmented lead-core line for deep-water trolling
- Weed-jigging methods

Two major walleye-fishing circuits in which thousands of anglers participate continued to place the spotlight on walleyes. Hence, the millions of anglers and NAFC Members who don't fish tournaments still benefit from these events. In addition to helping develop better fishing tackle, boats, motors and angling presentations, tournament anglers pay a conservation fee at each event. This money is used to promote walleye stocking efforts and other valuable conservation projects.

Money donated by tournament anglers has gone for projects ranging from building walleye-rearing ponds to catch-and-release management studies.

Management Tactics Spur Walleye Growth

Research and promotion of catch-and-release walleye management has proven that when properly handled, walleyes can be successfully caught, held in a livewell and later released with little chance of delayed mortality. Specific guidelines for safe handling of fish and improvements in livewell design resulted from this research.

This tournament angler steps out of his boat with the day's catch secure in a plastic bag. After his fish are weighed, they will be released unharmed to spawn and fight again. Tournaments and tournament anglers promote the wise use of fishing resources.

Boat manufacturers now build livewells that are better insulated and deeper in order to keep the water cool. Also, livewells have been moved from the front of the boat to the back where the fish receive a smoother ride. Sophisticated aeration and recirculation systems operated by timer-controlled switches are standard equipment on many of the better walleye boats.

Today, the live-release survival rate at most professionally managed walleye tournaments averages over 90 percent. For events held in early spring or late fall when the water is cooler and the oxygen level is higher, the successful catch-and-release rate often reaches 99 percent.

Walleye-fishing popularity has also spawned a new generation of conservation-minded anglers. Conservation and fisheries management efforts such as catch-and-release, selective harvest, slot limits and trophy management are on the lips of anglers and biologists everywhere.

The concept of selective harvest, for example, is seen as one of the most popular and beneficial management concepts in sportfishing. Selective harvest means that walleyes are both a valuable sportfish and an important food fish. By adhering to self-enforced guidelines to keep smaller fish and release larger adults, anglers can have their walleyes and eat them, too.

Complete Angler's Library

Slot limits accomplish the same goal, but are imposed by state or federal fisheries agencies and enforced by the agencies' conservation officials. Normally, slot limits allow an angler the opportunity to harvest a few small fish and one large, or trophy, fish per day. This form of harvest management prevents over-harvesting critical breeding stock while creating fishing opportunities for more anglers.

Unlike other species whose numbers dwindle in the face of increased fishing pressure, walleyes hold their own well. Given fairly normal conditions, walleyes not only survive, but thrive unlike any other species. Progressive fisheries management programs that balance supplemental stocking, natural reproduction and controlled sport harvest are helping to ensure high walleye populations in the best producing waters. This same management will create new walleye hotspots.

2

Understanding The Walleye's Biology

Walleyes are a favorite of fisheries biologists and anglers alike because they are easy to raise in hatchery situations, fast growing, adaptable to many different environments and provide undisputed sporting and eating qualities. In natural lakes, rivers and reservoirs, walleyes successfully inhabit a wider array of aquatic environments than northern pike, muskies, largemouth bass, stripers and many other popular species. Because of its rapidly expanding distribution, the walleye ranks near the top of the list of preferred sportfish with state fisheries personnel, tourism departments and many anglers.

Identifying Walleyes

A walleye is one of the easiest freshwater fish to identify unless the angler is fishing in waters which also hold the walleye's smaller cousin, the sauger, and the product of hybridization of the two species, a fish called the saugeye.

The walleye is the largest of the three species, with the sauger being the smallest, and only the walleye has a white spot on the caudal fin. The sauger has three to four dark saddles that cross the back of the fish, and rows of dark spots on the dorsal fins run parallel to the dorsal spines. The saugeyes grow larger than the sauger and some spotting occurs on the dorsal fin. The saugeye usually doesn't have the white tail marking of the walleye.

A widely distributed sportfish, walleyes are most abundant

This fat walleye is a product of its environment. Bodies of water that provide an abundant protein-rich forage base often produce fast-growing, potbellied specimens.

Understanding The Walleye's Biology   21

throughout southern Canada, the Great Lakes, the Upper Midwest and a few of the Western states. Extensive stocking efforts have doubled or tripled the walleye's natural distribution.

Many Eastern waters, including those of Pennsylvania, New York and Vermont, are boasting fast-growing walleye fisheries. Tennessee, Kentucky, Georgia, Missouri, Oklahoma and Texas are also future hotspots for the walleye.

Known by many local or regional names, walleyes are most often referred to as walleye pike or pickerel. Both names are misnomers, though, because walleyes are not related to either the northern pike or the chain pickerel.

The Spawning Period

Walleyes are among the first fish to spawn each spring. Even before the ice in northern waters has completely melted, walleyes begin migrating to and staging near traditional spawning grounds.

In some instances, walleyes migrate extreme distances to reach preferred spawning habitat. Fish that live in large river systems, such as the Mississippi, Illinois, Ohio and Missouri, have been reported to migrate hundreds of miles, traveling through several lock-and-dam systems along the way.

Dams stop the upstream migration of most pre-spawn walleyes, so spawning activity is usually concentrated in the tailrace area directly downstream of the dam or along riprap banks.

Reservoir walleyes react in much the same way as river-based fish. A well-defined upstream movement of fish occurs in most reservoir situations. Spawning usually occurs near dams, riprap banks or sand and gravel flats adjacent to the dam; however, in some reservoirs, creek arms are important spawning sites. Rocky points and shorelines attract spawn-laden walleyes.

Fish that live in natural lakes seek out reefs, shorelines and other shallow-water areas that feature bottoms consisting of scattered rock, gravel and sand.

Where walleyes spawn depends upon the type of habitat available to them. Gravel bottoms or areas of broken rock are preferred, but walleyes have been known to spawn on sand, clay and even among aquatic vegetation.

Walleyes also instinctively seem to choose areas that offer some form of current or flowing water which washes sediment from the eggs and provides a steady oxygen supply.

For years, anglers thought post-spawn female walleyes went through an uncatchable
recovery period. However, this angler proves
post-spawn walleyes can be found and pat-
terned. Many of these fish go deep after
spawning and can be caught by trolling various crankbaits and live-bait rigs.

Although most spawning activity takes place at night, in
deeper water some spawning may occur during daylight hours.

Exactly where female walleyes go after spawning is an often-
debated subject. Anglers traditionally have found it difficult to
locate and catch post-spawn females.

Understandably, many theories have developed in an attempt
to explain why adult females are difficult to catch during the post-
spawn period. The most popular theory suggests that females go
through a rest or recuperation period immediately after spawning.
During this period, the theory suggests that the females feed only
sparingly.

A more likely explanation is that walleyes disperse after
spawning to seek out badly picked-over populations of baitfish. By
late spring, the remaining baitfish have survived almost a year of
predation and disease. These numbers are slim at best, and the
walleyes must keep moving in order to find enough to eat.

Tournament walleye catches on Lake Erie indicate that post-
spawn walleyes seek out deep water. Large numbers of adult females are taken every year around the Bass-Islands region of Lake
Erie in 30 to 40 feet of water. Most are bottom-dwellers, but a few
suspend.

Readily taking the bait, these deep-water fish are obviously hungry and looking for an easy meal. If a post-spawn recovery period exists, odds are good it doesn't last long.

Similar findings in other fisheries support the theory that walleyes go deep in search of adult forage fish. Not all walleyes go deep, however. Smaller males remain on the spawning grounds for weeks after the last egg has been laid. Perhaps they are waiting for more females to arrive. No one knows why these males hang around the spawning grounds so long, but they are aggressive and easily caught.

Early Development

Once the eggs hatch, walleye fry feed on the egg sac for the first few days. When this available nutrition is exhausted, the fry are forced to find their food.

Tiny zooplankton are the major food source for the fry during the first few months of life. Young walleyes need a good supply of plankton in order to survive.

Once the young walleyes reach fingerling size they begin feeding heavily on small minnows and aquatic insect larva. By the end of the first summer, walleyes in fertile environments usually are 4 to 12 inches in length. Two-year-old fish average 12 to 16 inches in length, becoming adult fish during their third year.

The latitude of the waters in which walleyes live is a determinant of how quickly these fish mature and how long they live. It may take fish in northern climates four to five years to reach maturity, but they often will live 12 to 15 years.

In the South, walleyes grow much faster, reaching sexual maturity within three years; however, these fast-growing fish often live only six or seven years.

Diet also influences growth rates. Walleye populations that feed on protein-rich, soft-rayed forage fish grow faster and larger than fish that feed on less desirable forages. Soft-rayed forage fish—gizzard shad, alewives, smelt, emerald shiners, spottail shiners, fatheads, ciscoes, whitefish and suckers—are easier for walleyes to digest and turn into fish flesh. Less desirable forage species, including yellow perch, bluegills and bullheads, are more difficult for walleyes to catch and digest, so the resulting food value is less.

Adult Habits And Habitats

Describing all the habits and hangouts of the adult walleye

Walleye Food Preferences

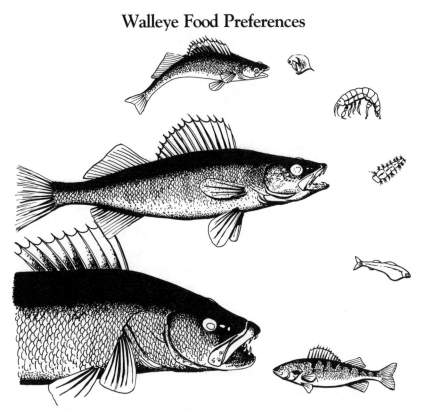

As walleyes mature, their taste in foods change. In the beginning stages of life (fry and finger-ling), they will eat daphnias and amphipods. While maturing, their preferences range from mos-quito larva to minnow-sized bait to young-of-the year yellow perch.

could easily fill an entire book. The walleye is a complex fish that survives and thrives in many different environments.

For years, biologists and anglers believed that the walleye was primarily a benthic (bottom-orientated) species. Even though walleyes are at home on classic bottom structure, such as sunken islands, reefs and submerged points, they are just as likely to be found in flooded timber, aquatic weeds or simply suspending in the water column.

Walleyes will take advantage of the best possible living ar-rangements. In large bodies of water offering many different envi-ronments, for example, walleyes often use several different eco-systems.

Aquatic weeds are a powerful attractant for walleyes. Weed cover attracts baitfish, making an excellent hunting ground for walleyes. Ambush feeders by nature, walleyes feed by darting out of cover and snapping up forage fish that stray too close.

Weeds not only offer cover but also camouflaging shade. The shade created by submerged cover helps the walleye blend into its environment, allowing it to approach forage species more easily while avoiding other predators. Walleyes also see better than baitfish in low-light conditions. Shade from submerged weeds provides an ideal walleye home.

Aquatic plants provide more cover and protection from predators than rock piles, reefs, points and other classic, walleye bottom structure. Not surprisingly, fisheries offering both habitat types will usually have more fish using the weeds.

Ironically, the highest fishing pressure centers upon areas that harbor the least number of fish. Those anglers who have discovered how to find and catch walleyes in weeds often enjoy fast-and-furious fishing action.

Like weeds, submerged wood serves as another important walleye habitat. Although not every river, reservoir or lake offers this type of cover for walleyes, those that do provide unique and exciting fisheries.

In rivers, submerged wood is usually concentrated in backwaters areas or near shorelines. Large rivers, like the Mississippi, feature huge backwaters or sloughs that harbor large numbers of walleyes. Walleyes that normally live in the main river channel frequently migrate into these sloughs during high-water periods. Flooded timber then becomes a strong magnet for these walleyes.

Reservoirs normally feature a lot of flooded timber. In some cases, the timber was harvested and removed before the reservoir was created. More often than not, however, standing timber was left to rot and decay naturally over a period of years. Barren trunks provide little in the way of shade and cover for walleyes, but bushy trees with lots of branches provide great cover. Fallen logs lying criss-crossed in the water also attract walleyes.

Submerged wood in natural lakes is usually found along the shoreline. Trees that have toppled into the water make excellent walleye cover, especially if there is a fairly steep drop-off near shore. Shorelines where the bottom tapers slowly into deep water will not attract many walleyes. Walleyes, like other predators, are reluctant to cross extensive, shallow flats, but wood cover adjacent to deep water is a major attractant.

Even though wood and weeds attract and hold large numbers of walleyes, under the right conditions, a portion of the walleye population in any lake and reservoir still will suspend in open water. In bodies of water that produce pelagic (suspended) forage species, such as smelt, alewives, shad, emerald shiners or ciscoes, walleyes often suspend far from bottom in order to feed upon these abundant baitfish.

Suspended walleyes are typically nomadic. Follow the movements of the baitfish to determine the whereabouts of these walleyes. A school of baitfish is seldom in the same place for long.

Although troublesome to locate and difficult to keep tabs on, suspended walleyes are fairly easy to catch. That's because suspended walleyes are much more likely to be feeding actively than those at the bottom.

Activity Day And Night

Few anglers would argue that walleyes bite better either early or late in the day. As crepuscular creatures, walleyes usually are most active when light levels are low, such as during twilight.

Preferring to hunt by using their sight advantage, walleyes also use their highly developed lateral-line sensory system to feed in total darkness. The lateral line acts like a radar system, picking up sounds and vibrations and deciphering them. Walleyes use this "sixth" sense to pinpoint the presence and travel direction of baitfish. Walleyes also use the lateral line to avoid predators.

3

At Home
Almost Anywhere

ccording to the time-worn cliche, "You are what you
eat," like people, fish are directly affected in their
overall health, growth rates, ability to resist disease
and reproductive powers by the type and quality of
food available. In short, a well-fed walleye population is more
likely to be healthy and able to thrive despite angling pressure.

This sounds simple to many anglers, but most of them have no
idea what constitutes a well-fed walleye population. The foods
walleyes feed upon change with the seasons and the various bodies
of water.

Walleye fry and immature fingerlings feed on certain foods;
adults depend upon a completely different forage. For a population of walleyes to grow and develop successfully, the body of water must contain all the links in the food chain.

The fact that walleyes are at home in lakes, rivers or reservoirs
is strong evidence that these fish are a very adaptable species. The
distribution, or range, of walleyes exceeds the range of all the important forage-fish species.

In Canadian Shield lakes, walleyes gorge on ciscoes, whitefish
and suckers; in the Great Lakes, alewife, emerald shiners and
smelt are on the menu, and in the larger rivers and reservoir systems of the nation's midsection, walleyes have ample supplies of
gizzard shad and threadfin shad. Meanwhile, smaller inland lakes
offer yellow perch, johnny darters and sticklebacks.

The actual forage species walleyes favor, however, is a strong

This young angler has learned that rivers and walleyes go hand in hand. In many smaller flows, casting from shore or wading is an excellent way to get consistent action.

At Home Almost Anywhere

topic of debate among numerous biologists and anglers. Many writers contend that walleyes and yellow perch epitomize the classic predator-prey relationship. Many anglers will make the claim that walleyes are rarely found far from their favorite food, the yellow perch.

The way these species interact in waters where they both thrive would seem obvious. However, there's strong evidence indicating walleyes often ignore abundant yellow perch in favor of soft-rayed forages, such as smelt, shad, alewife or ciscoes.

In 1986, the Michigan Department of Natural Resources conducted a stomach-content analysis to determine the types of forage species that walleyes favor in Saginaw Bay. The results of the research were a surprise to both biologists and anglers.

As part of the study, Michigan DNR boats set up a forage-base study to determine the relative populations of primary minnow species including spottail shiners, smelt, alewife, trout perch, gizzard shad and yearling yellow perch in the bay. Spottail shiners and young-of-the-year yellow perch were determined to be the most numerous forage species, but stomach-content analysis revealed that walleyes were feeding instead on soft-rayed alewife, smelt and gizzard shad. Test results showed that 40 percent of the walleye stomachs analyzed contained identifiable preyfish. Alewife (48 percent), smelt (28 percent) and gizzard shad (26 percent) were the predominant foods in the walleye stomachs!

Obviously, the walleyes were presented with an abundance of spottail shiners, yellow perch and other benthic forages, but they chose to feed primarily on pelagic (suspended) minnows. Biologists have theorized that these pelagic forage species are easier for walleyes to catch. It has also been suggested that walleyes instinctively know that these soft-rayed forages are higher in protein and easier to digest than spiny-rayed fish, such as johnny darters and yellow perch.

Saginaw Bay walleyes grow at an amazing rate. The average fish reaches a length of 20 inches (about 3 to 4 pounds) within three years. While the Saginaw Bay forage study is only one example of selective feeding by walleyes, indications are that this type of feeding behavior occurs in many other fisheries. To understand the connection between forage and walleyes, anglers must analyze individual bodies of water.

As previously mentioned, the types of forage common in

This tagged walleye is ready to be set free. Information learned from tagged fish has helped biologists predict the seasonal movements, growth rates and preferred haunts of walleyes across the nation. Continued research assures learning many exciting walleye habits and behaviors.

shield lakes are much different from the forage found in the Great Lakes, rivers or other inland lakes. Each body of water provides a unique food chain beginning with the smallest zooplankton and ending with primary predators, such as walleyes.

The Food Chain Pyramid

Various units of the food chain and their relative abundance stack up like a pyramid. At the bottom of the food chain, or pyramid, millions of tiny zooplankton provide forage for insects, newly hatched fish and other small aquatic creatures. The same aquatic animals that feed on plankton are themselves food for minnows, small fish and crustaceans.

Moving up the pyramid, larger gamefish eat minnows, immature gamefish, crayfish and other aquatic animals. At the top of

At Home Almost Anywhere   31 the food pyramid, the number of primary predators is relatively small compared to the zooplankton population at the pyramid's bottom. These fish survive by feeding on smaller adult fish, minnows, aquatic insects and crustaceans.

In many waters, walleyes are prey for northern pike, muskies or larger walleyes. The forage base in every body of water is different. Although certain waters have similar forage makeups, subtle but important differences make each body of water unique.

Trophy fisheries are a good example of waters that offer well-balanced forage bases. Certain lakes produce excellent numbers of trophy-class fish, while similar waters produce nothing but small and average-sized fish. Differences in genetic strains account for some of the difference; however, available forage also affects the production of trophy-sized walleyes. For a fishery to produce maximum numbers of fish in all size classes, all levels of the food pyramid must be present and healthy.

A missing link in the food chain burdens fish, making it difficult for them to grow beyond a specific size. Lakes that produce a lot of small walleyes but few adult-sized fish are common in many regions. Missing forage prevents immature fish from getting the nutrition they need to reach large sizes.

The Mayfly

Biologists believe the common mayfly is the missing link in the food chain of many fisheries. A delicate insect, a mayfly larva burrows into the lake bottom until it's fully developed. Once the larva develops, the adult insect exits its burrow and swims to the surface. At the surface, the insect splits its outer skeleton and escapes into the air like a butterfly ridding itself of its cocoon.

During an active mayfly hatch, millions of these flying insects cloud the sky. Discarded skeletons litter the water's surface and beaches.

During their hatches, mayflies—often referred to as fishflies or lakeflies—provide a valuable food source for other aquatic creatures, such as panfish and immature walleyes. Biologists theorize that the decline of the common mayfly in some areas is a major reason why walleye growth rates are often stunted. Even though there are huge numbers of young walleyes in these waters, the immature fish never seem to grow to respectable adult size.

The mayfly is an important forage link for immature and adult

Pyramid Food Chain

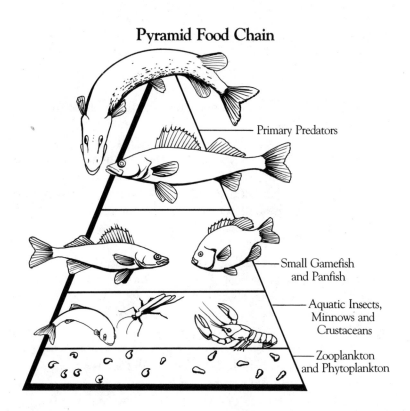

Primary Predators

Small Gamefish
and Panfish

Aquatic Insects,
Minnows and
Crustaceans

Zooplankton
and Phytoplankton

The food pyramid represents the food chain existing in different environments. This pyramid reflects the aquatic environment. A missing link in the chain causes certain species to remain small. Many biologists believe the common mayfly, within the aquatic insect category, is the missing link in many fisheries.

walleyes alike. Young-of-the-year walleyes are often too small to feed on adult minnows, but too big to depend upon a zooplankton diet. Mayfly larvae are the ideal step in the food chain for these particular fish.

There are indications that the decline of the mayfly may be linked to contaminated bottom sediments. Chemical contaminants from paper mills, power plants, chemical factories and other industrial factories eventually settle in the bottom sediments in which the mayfly larvae burrow.

Important Forage Species

While the mayfly and other aquatic insects are important parts of the walleye diet, minnows and other small fish make up the bulk of the walleye diet.

Depending upon the latitude, one of several shad species is likely to be an important walleye forage. In the northern part of the United States, gizzard shad are a prominent forage species in rivers, reservoirs, the Great Lakes and other large bodies of water. Farther south, the threadfin shad and gizzard shad are important walleye forage species.

Both species are delicate creatures susceptible to rapid changes in water temperature. Huge die-offs often occur when there are rapid changes in water temperature.

In the northern part of the gizzard shad's range, these periodic die-offs are common. If it weren't for the prolific nature of this species, gizzard shad probably wouldn't be able to survive in northern latitudes.

Natural die-offs keep most shad small. Although these fish frequently grow too large to be walleye prey, most shad only live long enough to become perfect-sized snacks for walleyes.

Gizzard shad do not feed on plankton like other species of minnows. This unique species feeds on plants and other organic matter scoured from the bottom. Because gizzard shad transform plant material directly into fish flesh, these small fish are a vital forage base in many rivers and large bodies of water.

Unfortunately for anglers, the gizzard shad makes a poor live bait. A delicate minnow, the shad dies quickly in a minnow bucket and on the end of a hook.

Alewife and rainbow smelt are two saltwater fish that were accidentally introduced to the Great Lakes. Believed to be a primary reason for the decline of natural Great Lakes forage species, including lake herring and chubs, these unwanted fish have become both a nuisance and a blessing in the Great Lakes ecosystem.

During the mid-1960s, enormous die-offs of alewives soiled miles of public beaches along Lake Michigan and prompted the first planting of Pacific salmon to help control these pests. Coho and king salmon were introduced into the lakes and within a few short years a world-class sportfishery developed. Alewives and smelt provided an ideal forage for salmon and have become an important forage for Great Lakes walleyes, as well.

Rainbow smelt have also been introduced in many fisheries as forage fish. The many reservoir systems along the Missouri River are prime examples. Many clearwater lakes in the western and northeastern part of the country also harbor smelt.

The most widespread, walleye-forage species is the common fathead minnow. Fatheads, raised by the billions in hatcheries, thrive in almost any type of environment. They are extremely adaptable, as well as an attractive baitfish for finicky walleyes.

An important forage species, smelt make excellent tablefare, and tons of smelt are harvested commercially. When pan-fried the bones in smelt soften and can be eaten. Although dead and frozen smelt are sometimes used as fish bait, walleye fishermen seldom use smelt.

The common fathead minnow is undoubtedly the most widespread of all the common walleye forage species. Easily raised in commercial hatcheries, fatheads are reared by the billions for use as fish bait.

Fathead minnows are commonly introduced into waters that lack suitable forage species. A very adaptable minnow, the fathead will thrive in a wide variety of environments. These unique fish spawn by depositing their eggs under boards or other flat objects in the water. During the spawning season, the male develops a pad on its back which is used to clean the eggs deposited by the female.

The use of fatheads as bait has undoubtedly contributed to the growing distribution of this species. A hardy minnow, the fathead thrives in environments that would quickly kill other minnows.

After fishing a tournament on the Illinois River, an angler found himself with a bucket full of frisky fatheads. Rationalizing that healthy minnows like these were just too good to throw out, he poured the minnows into the livewell of his boat, along with another half pail of water.

Upon reaching home, he promptly forgot about the minnows in the livewell. Two weeks later, while preparing the boat for another trip, he remembered the fatheads.

When he opened the livewell, he expected to find a stinking mess. Instead, his livewell was full of healthy and happy fathead minnows. Not a minnow had died, despite not having clean water or aeration. Fatheads are tough minnows!

The spottail shiner may not be as hardy as the fathead minnow, but these bottom-dwelling minnows are among the most common walleye forages. Preferring to live on sand, gravel or rock bottoms, the spottail shiner is a silvery minnow with a distinctive dark spot at the base of the caudal fin.

The spottail spawns in the mouths of rivers and streams. Not surprisingly, spottail shiners are among the first readily available forages that river-bound walleyes encounter after their own spawning rituals. River mouths attract spawning spottail shiners at about the same time that post-spawn walleyes are heading downstream looking for an easy meal.

A popular live bait, spottails are easily kept alive as long as the water in the minnow bucket is kept cool.

Another benthic minnow, the johnny darter is actually a member of the Percidae, or perch, family. It is a small minnow, rarely exceeding 4 inches in length. Over 95 species of darter minnows inhabit the United States and Canada.

Abundant in many rivers and natural lakes, these minnows prefer cool and clear waters. During the spring spawning season, darters display brilliant pink, red and yellow colors contrasting with their overall dark bodies. Darters are the primary walleye forage in many northern lakes; yet these small minnows rarely show up in a minnow bucket. Staying tight to the bottom, these minnows are difficult to net or capture in traps.

Don't Forget Suckers

No discussion of walleye forages would be complete without a few words about the common sucker. Abundant almost everywhere walleyes are caught, small suckers make an ideal walleye forage.

Although adult suckers are in no danger of becoming a walleye's breakfast, young-of-the-year suckers provide an excellent source of protein for hungry walleyes. Found in lakes, rivers and reservoirs, suckers are a common bait species.

Small suckers can be found at almost any bait shop in walleye areas. The sucker minnow's rubbery mouth holds a fish hook unlike any other baitfish. Popular with anglers who cast jigs or spoons, a sucker will stay securely pinned to a jig for many casts.

Other Forage

While only a few of the most common forage species are outlined in these pages, hundreds of other minnows and small fish are prime targets for hungry walleyes. Ciscoes or lake herring are important forages in northern lakes. Sculpins, emerald shiners, golden shiners, sticklebacks, dace minnows and young-of-the-year freshwater drum are just a few other species that commonly end up in walleye stomachs.

Understanding the forage connection and how it relates to walleyes is an important aspect of sportfishing. Learning the types of forage fish present in a fishery, and the habits of those species, can point the angler in the direction of walleyes. After all, walleyes are what they eat. Finding walleyes to catch is no more difficult than locating their preferred forages.

Tackle And Equipment Trends

4

'Just Right' Walleye Boat

Perfect walleye fishing boats exist only in the minds of the anglers who own them. The fact that no two anglers fish exactly alike proves that building the perfect walleye boat is impossible. The ideal walleye fishing boat is even difficult to imagine. Overall size, construction material, design, brand and many other variables are not easily blended into a manufacturing melting pot that pours out a boat which every angler considers to be an ideal fishing craft.

Life isn't that simple and neither is selecting a fishing boat designed to chase walleyes. The angling methods an angler uses, the types of waters he fishes, the amount of money he can invest and, to some degree, his personal preference help determine which boat is indeed the "just right" walleye boat for the consumer.

A Brief History Of Fishing Boats

To say that fishing boats have changed in recent years is a serious understatement. The introduction and popularity of the bass boat in the early '70s sparked a movement in boat design that left a lasting impact on anglers everywhere.

Species-specific boats made a tremendous splash with anglers and the marine industry. The trend started with bass boats and eventually expanded to rigs designed for walleye, crappie and striper fishing. Others are sure to follow. However, no fishing craft has evolved more in the last decade than the walleye boat.

Boats used for walleye fishing in the early 1980s were typically

Species-specific boats have been the latest craze in sportfishing. Starting with bass boats, the marine industry has manufactured several models for different species, including walleyes. This walleye boat is expertly rigged to fit almost any type of walleye-fishing situation.

14- to 16-foot aluminum crafts powered by small outboard motors. Boats with motors larger than 40 horsepower were rare. Small boats and small motors may have continued to dominate the walleye fishing scene if it weren't for tournaments and the anglers who compete in them. Walleye pioneers, including Bob Propst, Mike McClelland, Gary Roach, Gary Parsons and Jerry Anderson, had a lot to do with influencing the evolution of the now-popular walleye-fishing boats.

Common sense dictated that chasing walleyes in large wind-swept lakes, such as the Great Lakes and reservoirs, called for bigger and safer boats. Increasing the size and horsepower rating on these rigs enabled anglers to power through rough water with more ease and safety.

The added advantage of mobility on calm water quickly became a factor in tournament fishing. Anglers equipped with larger and faster boats easily covered more water while hunting for fish. The results were obvious and dramatic. Interest in maintaining a competitive edge stimulated these anglers to demand even larger and more powerful walleye rigs.

Gradually, the trend toward bigger and better boats resulted in the high-performance walleye fishing boats of the early 1990s. The latest top-of-the-line walleye boat is a far cry from the tipsy aluminum skiffs of the '80s. Bigger, wider, faster, safer and, of course, more expensive, the "just right" walleye boat is from 17 to 20 feet in length, carries a 90- to 175-horsepower rating and offers the angler top speeds in excess of 60 miles per hour on calm water.

Buying A Walleye Boat

Purchasing a walleye boat is a serious undertaking. A lot of thought, planning and evaluation must be done in order for the owner to be satisfied and happy with the product.

The process of selecting an ideal boat for each customer is a complicated one. Potential boat buyers often walk into marine showrooms with preconceived ideas regarding the affordability, overall quality and resale value of various boat brands. Such notions are potentially dangerous to the boat buyer who closes his mind to all the available options, often making it impossible to get the best possible buy!

Size, affordability, model, brand and the boat's physical make-up make a boat-buying decision complicated. Selection of the

The trend in walleye boats is toward larger and faster open-water models, such as the side-console model; however, smaller backtroller models continue to sell in northern regions of the country. Side-console boats are noted for being good rough-water boats.

ideal boat by each customer requires a tedious but necessary process of eliminating models, adding options and compromising on features until the buyer can make the best possible choice.

Yes, compromising. Purchase of most family fishing boats results in compromise. Many fishing rigs take on another function as weekend and vacation-time pleasure crafts, such as pulling water skiers, for example. Selecting a boat that meets all criteria is no easy task.

Size Considerations

Is bigger really better? Are the larger and roomier boats worth the extra cash? Marine dealers face these questions almost every time they talk with a perspective customer.

Bigger, faster and seaworthier boats have earned an important niche in the world of walleye-fishing boats. Unfortunately, these deluxe models often come with "deluxe" price tags to match. In many cases, top-of-the-line walleye rigs represent more boat than necessary for the average angler.

The goal in selecting a walleye-fishing boat should be to end up with a product that best suits the many needs of the angler.

The types of waters most commonly fished, the number of persons the boat can hold comfortably and the area available for storing the boat during the off-season are just a few of the important considerations that must be weighed when deciding upon boat size.

Many anglers make the mistake of starting out too small so they quickly outgrow their boats. On the other hand, buying a large boat that's more difficult to trailer, handle on the water and store may not be the best choice, either.

A serious walleye angler has many boats to choose from ranging in size from 16 to 20 feet in length. Small- to medium-sized (16 to 17 feet) boats are best suited for use on protected waters or when only two or three anglers will be fishing from them. The larger, 18- to 20-foot boats are better equipped to handle big expanses of water, rougher seas and larger fishing parties.

Fiberglass Vs. Aluminum

The age-old battle of fiberglass vs. aluminum boats is waged across walleye land. Which boat-building material is best? It's safe to say that fiberglass boats don't receive the consideration they deserve.

Aluminum and fiberglass boats each have advantages and disadvantages. Unfortunately, many anglers never look beyond stereotypes in order to discover the benefits of fiberglass hulls.

Two misconceptions regarding fiberglass boats run rampant among fishermen. Most anglers are convinced that fiberglass hulls are considerably heavier than comparably sized aluminum hulls. Not true. The misconception is that fiberglass boats are fragile and need special care.

Overall boat weight is a factor that's not influenced solely by hull material. How the boat is built and what goes inside the outer skin ultimately determines how heavy the final product will be in the end.

Comparable aluminum and fiberglass fishing boats are closer in weight than many anglers realize. This is especially true of larger boats which require more reinforcement and bracing in order to withstand the punishment of being pushed through rough water by powerful outboards. The most popular 17-foot aluminum boat on the market, for example, weighs approximately 850 pounds. A comparable fiberglass rig would tip the scales at approximately 900 pounds.

Pro fisherman Gary Roach prefers an 18-foot backtroller boat. The extra room makes it possible for several persons to fish in comfort. Roach equips his boats with a 90-horsepower, tiller-controlled outboard, 9.9 horsepower kicker motor and a transom-mounted electric trolling motor.

Another common fallacy is that fiberglass hulls are fragile and easily damaged. Fiberglass is a strong yet flexible boat-building material. Glass also has the added advantage of being easily repaired if damaged.

A fiberglass hull can be repaired by any good body-shop technician. A damaged area can be quickly repaired by covering it with additional fiberglass matte and layers of gelcoat or fiberglass resin. Several layers of resin are laid and allowed to dry thoroughly. The final layers of gelcoat are pigmented to match the exact color of the boat. Excess gelcoat is feathered out with fine grit sandpaper and the finished product then is buffed, waxed and polished.

A craftsman skilled in fiberglass repair can work magic on a damaged boat. On the other hand, repairing damage to aluminum hulls is a more complicated process. Returning a damaged aluminum hull to its original condition is next to impossible.

The old adage that aluminum boats are tough on the rocks is dangerously false. No boat is built to withstand running ashore or colliding with sunken rocks and debris. Aluminum and fiberglass boats will both suffer from this type of treatment. The big difference, however, is in repairing the damage.

Another hidden advantage of fiberglass is that it can be

molded into virtually any shape imaginable. Therefore, glass hulls have led the way in performance design.

Fiberglass fishing-boat hulls offer smoother, dryer and more comfortable rides in all types of wave action. Most glass boats feature a reversed-chime hull that cuts through waves, forcing the water and spray to either side. In comparison, aluminum hulls are boxy in shape and tend to plow water instead of cutting through it. The broad bow of an aluminum hull forces spray upward at the point where the boat's forward motion collides with the water, soaking the occupants.

Structural limitations prevent aluminum from being formed into reversed-chime hulls or the padded-style hulls found on the fastest bass and walleye boats. Padded fiberglass hulls are actually designed to bring most of the boat out of the water when it's running at full or near-full speed. Only a small pad near the back of the boat remains in the water when the craft is on plane. Padded hulls provide more lift, less drag and far greater top-end speeds.

Aluminum boats ride on the point of the v-bottom hull at all speeds. The hull's increased surface area which is in contact with the water prevents aluminum-hull boats from reaching their maximum speeds, even when equipped with high-horsepower engines.

The overall appearance of fiberglass boats is a final consideration. Multi-colored gelcoats and special finishes, such as metal flaking, add flash, color and style to fiberglass hulls. Aluminum boats depend upon standard paint jobs for a pleasing look.

Despite all the merits of fiberglass-hulled fishing boats, aluminum boat sales continue to far outnumber fiberglass hulls purchased for walleye fishing.

Choosing A Tiller Or Side-Console Model

Deciding on a tiller model or a console (steering wheel) version fishing boat is a serious stumbling block for many anglers. Traditionally, tiller-model fishing boats have been considered the choice of serious anglers. The influence of tournament fishing giants has affected this angling attitude.

Tiller rigs and backtrolling angling for which they were designed are popular in the heartland of walleye fishing. (Minnesota, Wisconsin, North Dakota, South Dakota and Nebraska). Chasing walleyes in these heartland states is more than a pastime—it's a cult-like activity.

The need for speed in tournaments inspired pro angler Gary Parsons to switch to a console rig, while most used tiller-controlled rigs. Parsons designed his boat's transom to accept a small, gasoline kicker motor. He uses the small motor for all his backtrolling and forward trolling chores; the larger one simply gets him to his hotspot quickly.

Most of the current knowledge of walleyes and walleye fishing came from these states, so it stands to reason that tiller fishing boats are still popular in this heartland.

Despite the enormous popularity of backtroller rigs, many anglers are making the switch to side-console fishing boats. Side-console rigs feature larger horsepower rating, greater top-end speeds and more recreational flexibility.

Walleye-fishing professional Gary Parsons of Chilton, Wisconsin, is credited with designing the first serious side-console walleye-fishing boat. Parsons calls it a side-console/backtrolling concept in walleye boats.

"I didn't invent a third category of fishing boats," says Parsons. "I simply set out to combine the best features of a tiller and side-console rig into a single boat that can be controlled from front or back."

A side-console/backtroller rig has a large outboard motor for speed, along with a specially designed transom that accepts a small 9.9- or 15-horsepower kicker motor. The small gasoline motor is used to control the boat when the operator uses trolling or backtrolling techniques.

Most side-console/backtrolling rigs are equipped with a main engine ranging in horsepower from 100 to 175. Adding bow- and

The ideal walleye boat should be deep enough to withstand rough water, have a v-hull to cut through rough waves and range in size from 17 to 19 feet in length.

Complete Angler's Library

transom-mounted electric motors provides even more boat-control options.

"Most side-console/backtrolling boats are designed with a deep splash well that enables the angler to backtroll into waves without adding splash or wave guards," adds Parsons. "When fishing from a side-console/backtroller boat, the angler has many boat-control options available to him. The boat can be controlled with a bow-mounted electric motor, a transom-mounted electric motor or a more powerful, gasoline kicker motor."

The angling presentation chosen dictates which method of boat control is best. Backtrolling live-bait rigs into bumpy seas and forward-trolling presentations, such as crankbaiting with planer boards, are tailor-made for the kicker motor. In calm water, the angler may prefer to use a bow-mounted electric motor to scoot along the shoreline while casting jigs or crankbaits. Rigging weedlines in gin-clear northern lakes calls for the control and silence of a transom-mounted electric motor.

"A fully rigged side-console/backtroller boat is capable of performing every imaginable boat-control chore," says Parsons. "More importantly, the side-console/backtroller boat is a faster, smoother and more versatile family fishing/recreation boat."

Choosing the "just right" walleye boat is a difficult task, indeed. Big boats, small boats, fiberglass models and aluminum versions and tillers and console rigs all have their niche. The list of brand options and equipment gets larger every season.

5

Boat Rigging, Trailering, Maintenance

Most anglers agree that boat-rigging chores are details that the marine dealer should worry about. After all, this is not the subject anglers usually sit around discussing over coffee; however, the way a walleye boat is rigged can have a dramatic effect on the overall comfort and fishability of the final product.

The more complicated facets of boat rigging, such as hanging engines and adjusting steering cables and wiring electronics, are best left to a trusted marine dealer. However, many rigging decisions including the placement of rod holders, fishing electronics, transducers, kicker motors, electric motors and, of course, batteries are details the wise boat buyer should not ignore.

Rigging a new boat is fun and helps the angler add a personal touch to his or her boat. More importantly, doing the final rigging chores helps guarantee that your boat will be a comfortable and more efficient fishing machine when it hits the water.

Before getting out your tools, you should launch your new boat and get an idea how it floats at rest. Many of the new deep-v walleye rigs are heavy in back because of the weight that a large outboard and kicker motor add to the transom. For the best steering, tracking and high-speed running capabilities that the hull has to offer, transom-heavy boats must be counter-balanced so they will set level in the water.

Glass boats require special attention to weight distribution because they don't have an exposed keel like an aluminum hull. The

Weight Distribution

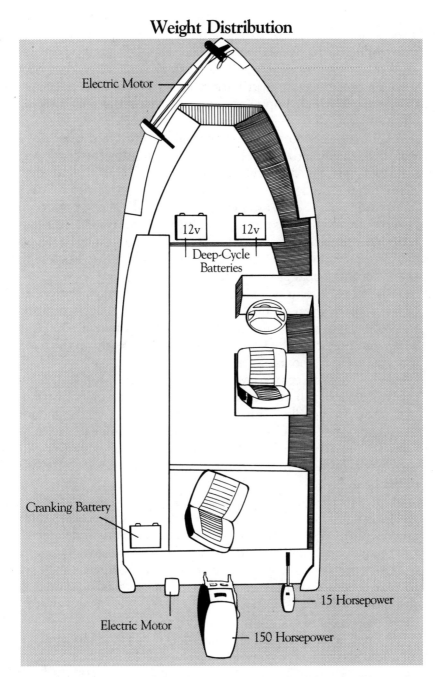

Electric Motor

12v   12v

Deep-Cycle Batteries

Cranking Battery

Electric Motor

15 Horsepower

150 Horsepower

*Weight distribution, or how a boat sits at rest in the water, can make or break boat perfor-
mance. If a boat is back-heavy, it may not plane out properly. Too much weight on one side
could cause the boat to tilt; too much weight forward causes a boat to plow water.*

Boat Rigging, Trailering, Maintenance   51

keel on an aluminum boat helps the boat turn sharply and track true while drifting. Glass boats make up for not having a protruding keel by floating level with the water's surface. A glass boat with the proper weight distribution has a greater hull surface area in the water which improves the craft's handling and tracking abilities.

Adding heavy outboard motors and batteries to the back of a glass boat can disturb this delicate balance, ruining the boat's performance. Heavy, deep-cycle, trolling-motor batteries are normally mounted near the bow to help level out transom-heavy boats. Many of the larger walleye rigs require the added power of a 24-volt electric trolling motor. Finding space for two 12-volt batteries near the front of the boat isn't always easy. It may be necessary to mount one battery in a dry well and the other as close to the front of the boat as possible.

It's imperative to secure these batteries to the boat's floor to prevent them from sliding around when the boat is running through rough water. Unfortunately, batteries take a pounding when mounted near the bow. Still, the added weight in the front is a must for most boats.

Achieving correct weight distribution doesn't stop with placing trolling-motor batteries forward. Side-to-side weight distribution must also be taken into consideration. Most anglers mount the gasoline-fueled kicker motors on the console-side of the transom. To offset this extra 100 pounds, secure a main engine cranking battery in the rear battery compartment on the opposite side of the boat.

The bow-mounted electric motor should be on the port side of the gunwale, helping balance off the weight of the kicker motor and operator. A transom-mounted electric motor is added opposite the gasoline kicker to further distribute weight evenly.

Once the weight is distributed properly, the console can be set up with a complete array of gauges and electronics. Mounted in the dashboard are a trim gauge, tachometer, speedometer, water-pressure gauge and engine-temperature gauge.

A high-quality liquid crystal graph or paper graph unit is mounted on top of the console conveniently for the boat's driver to operate. Two transducers for this unit are mounted on the back of the boat. A wide-angle (45-degree) transducer is installed to mark suspended or spooky fish, and a 192-kHz (20-degree) trans-

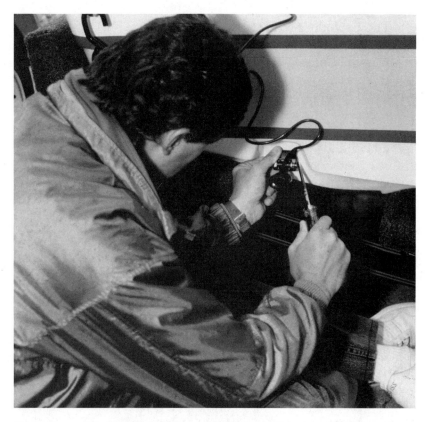

The author carefully mounts a transducer on his new walleye boat. Most problems with sonar units can be attributed to improper transducer installation.

ducer is mounted to mark fish holding tight to the bottom.

A dependable compass easily seen from the back of the boat should be mounted next to the graph. The compass is used with the GPS/plotter or loran/plotter. This allows an angler to follow trolling routes precisely. Also, the compass brings the angler home if the GPS or loran system fails.

Next, rig the bow platform with electronics. Most anglers prefer a high-resolution liquid crystal unit, but flashers are also popular. A puck-type transducer attaches to the bottom of the electric trolling motor and a transducer switch box is installed enabling the angler on the bow, with a flip of the switch, to instantly read water depths and fish marks from the boat's front or back. This is especially handy when fishing steep breaklines or structure that require precise boat control.

The bow-mounted LCG unit's placement is critical. Mount the graph on the top-side of the deck where it is highly visible. Many anglers mount their forward locators on the carpeted front deck. This low mounting position makes it difficult for an angler to watch his graph closely at all times. It also takes up valuable floor space.

Attach sonar units on heavy-duty-model swivel mounts. The mounts intended for use with bulky paper graphs are best because they can withstand the jarring from the boat running in rough water better than smaller mounts. Nothing is worse than having your expensive graph fly off the bow when the boat crashes into a wave.

A boat rein (retractable mooring rope) mounted in the boat's bow is handy for anglers who commonly launch their boats alone. It can be attached to the trailer during launching, eliminating the need for an extra rope tied on the bow eye. A couple more boat reins mounted on the side rails are also handy. Be sure to mount these devices where they can be easily reached for maintenance purposes.

A third graph placed near the boat's transom helps when the angler is backtrolling, drifting or rigging with slip weights. Many of the better walleye rigs have an extra electronics box mounted near the transom to make fishing off the back of the boat more convenient. In this box, a second liquid crystal graph or flasher is mounted with a 192-kHz and 50-kHz transducer. The 192-kHz transducer is used when fishing precise structure and pinpoint boat control is critical. The wide-angle, 50-kHz transducer is helpful for marking suspended fish.

Also mounted in this rear box is a VHF radio. The mounting location of VHF radios is a personal choice; however, this piece of equipment usually gets the most use while you're fishing—not while traveling to and from fishing areas. If the VHF radio is mounted on the console, it is difficult to reach while you're running the kicker or transom-mounted electric motor. Make sure to keep this in mind when deciding on its location.

Mounting rod holders is another important consideration. It's important to place these accessories properly the first time in order to avoid drilling unnecessary holes in the boat. At least eight rod holders will be needed at strategic spots along the boat's inside rail. Mount the first rod holder on the splash well, close to the kicker motor. When you're operating the kicker motor, you will

When mounting rod holders, be sure to put them in the proper location. They should be placed where seats, boat lids and other fishing accessories won't interfere with their smooth operation.

find this rod holder perfectly placed if you need both hands free in order to tie up a rig or deal with a snagged rod.

Directly opposite from the kicker motor, two more rod holders are mounted approximately 3 feet apart. Both rod holders are close enough to the back of the boat so the person operating the kicker motor or transom electric can easily reach them. These rod holders are handy for structure trolling or fishing with planer boards; they also work during drift fishing.

Finally, two more rod holders are positioned between the kicker-motor operator's seat and the console. These holders must frequently be placed fairly close together because of limited space. Be sure to space them far enough apart so each holder can rotate properly.

Although eight holder locations are utilized, it's only necessary to purchase six complete rod holders and two extra mounting bases. The rod holder heads then can be placed wherever needed, depending upon which type of presentation the angler is using.

Choose A Good Trailer

Although few anglers give it much thought, a dependable trailer to haul your boat is an important choice. Most marine dealers put their boats on inexpensive trailers in order to keep the to-

Lubricate wheel bearings twice a year to help prevent bearing wear and failure. Most trailers come with bearing protectors as standard equipment. If your trailer doesn't have protectors, they can be purchased and easily installed.

tal cost of the boat/motor/trailer package down. In the long run, paying a few dollars more for a quality trailer can save a lot of wear and tear on your boat.

Bunk-style trailers are cheap insurance against hull damage when towing boats long distances. Aluminum boats are especially vulnerable to the hull stress and damage that can result from trailering boats long distances. Look for a trailer that has large, car-sized tires. Oversized tires provide your boat with a smoother ride and hold the road better at highway speeds.

Auxiliary braking systems, such as surge or electric brakes, are also extremely helpful. These systems are dependable and can effectively reduce braking distance. Surge brakes are mounted on the trailer tongue and automatically begin braking the moment the towing vehicle slows. A slight clunk is heard each time the breaking system engages and disengages.

Electric brakes also work well, but they must be wired into the towing vehicle. If the boat will be towed by more than one vehicle, surge brakes are probably a better choice.

Custom, bunk-style trailers add to the boat's overall appearance and resale value. Available in colors to match almost any boat, a good trailer adds the "finishing touch" to any first-rate fishing boat.

Finally, a few minutes of preseason preparation will help guarantee a season full of trouble-free trailering. Greasing the wheel bearings and checking all the tires is a must each and every season. Anglers traveling long distances with their rigs should pack the bearings twice a year.

The popular bearing protectors, considered standard equipment on many trailers, are extremely helpful to busy fishermen. Simply keeping these special waterproof hubs full of grease eliminates most bearing-wear problems.

Even with bearing protectors, it's a good idea to remove, check and pack the bearing with grease by hand at least once a year. Bearing protectors don't always grease the inner bearings adequately. A greasy job once a year is well worth the hassle.

6

Making The Most Of Fishing Electronics

Thank goodness for depthfinders. Without these marvels of the modern fishing era, sportfishing as it is known today would not be possible. Electronic "fishfinders," as many anglers refer to them, completely revolutionized the fishing scene in the early '60s. Thirty years later, anglers are still learning about sonar and the science of developing better and easier ways to use fishing electronics.

Technological advances have come a long way, but in the evolutionary scheme of things, the technology used in fishing electronics is still in its infancy. Every year depthfinder manufacturers dramatically improve products and make new headway in developing more advanced units.

Purchasing and getting the most from fishing electronics has become a confusing game and a frustrating struggle for the average fisherman. Dozens of manufacturers are building and marketing fishing sonar, and every company claims that its product is the best on the market. Although most manufacturers have the technology to develop and produce outstanding fishing electronics, not all the products in the marketplace live up to the advertisers' claims.

For the serious walleye fisherman, quality electronics are absolutely necessary. Before buying fishing electronics, however, an angler should talk with other knowledgeable anglers and dealers to get their opinions on fishing sonar.

Visiting a tournament weigh-in is one of the best ways to in-

The evolution of depthfinders has been dramatic in recent years. One of the first units available was the flasher. This unit can be extremely effective when placed next to the driver's seat; it scouts bottom structure when the boat is moving at high speed.

Making The Most Of Fishing Electronics

vestigate sonar equipment. The first thing the angler will notice is that most tournament competitors outfit their boats with two, three or even four sonar units!

Even though it might seem like overkill, having several types of sonar at the angler's fingertips provides some valuable options. For example, a flasher mounted near the driver's seat is handy for scouting out bottom structure when the boat is traveling at high speeds. Running with the flasher on is a great way to locate sunken islands, reefs, underwater points, weeds and other structure or cover that attract walleyes. Many of the best fishing structure and cover are not marked on maps. The best way to find these areas is with a flasher.

Keep in mind that a flasher marks changes in bottom contour and fish almost instantaneously, making this form of sonar tops at high-speed operation. There's a three- to seven-second delay from the time rebounded sound waves are received until they print out on an LCG or paper-graph screen.

Once productive-looking structure is located, an LCG or paper graph can be used to slowly and thoroughly scan the bottom for signs of walleyes. Because LCG units don't require expensive graph paper, they are more economical to use.

Nothing works for scanning precise sections of the bottom or fish that are holding tight to the bottom as well as a paper graph. A confidence builder of sorts, a paper graph provides a permanent printout of structure, cover and fish.

Having more than one sonar unit on board helps the operator position the boat more accurately when fishing fast-sloping breaks, river wing dams or small pieces of bottom structure. Two anglers fishing and observing sonar units at opposite ends of the boat can easily determine the optimum fish-catching position.

Even a single angler can accomplish the same goal by installing transducer switch boxes on his boat. With a transducer switch box, an angler can obtain signals from two different transducers on a single graph. In other words, an angler fishing off the bow can scan water near the transom by simply flipping a switch activating a transom-mounted transducer.

Regardless of the type of sonar unit purchased—flasher, paper graph, video recorder or liquid crystal graph—each unit operates basically the same as the others. However, there's much more to know when it comes to using sonar effectively to locate walleyes.

The paper graph receives little attention since the introduction of LCG units. However, no other fishing sonar unit, including flashers, LCGs and video display units, can compete with the resolution provided by paper graphs.

Unfortunately, getting the most out of any depthfinder requires some effort on the angler's part. Sure, fishing electronics have come a long way, but they're not magic underwater windows (not yet at least) that tell you everything you need to know about fish location.

The most expensive and sophisticated fishing electronics on the market can't find fish. They can only show fish that the angler has found. Certainly, sonar makes it much easier to find the areas that fish frequent. In essence, fishermen use sonar to locate bottom structure and cover that attract fish. If walleyes are at home, their presence will be indicated on a good unit. That's important, but remember even the best sonar devices are only scanning a small circle beneath the boat at any given moment.

Sound waves emitted from the transducer disperse into the

water in a cone shape, and the transducer's cone angle determines the amount of bottom being scanned.

Transducers featuring narrow cone angles (as low as 8 degrees) operate with high-frequency (192 to 200 kHz) sound waves, so the resolution, or detail, provided is very acute. Wide-angle transducers (up to 45 degrees) send a lower-frequency (50 kHz) sound wave that penetrates deep water better. Because of the wider pulse width of the sound wave, however, these units aren't capable of providing as much resolution.

It's a trade-off: detailed resolution or wider bottom coverage. Which is better and what transducer cone angle is the best for the walleye fisherman? In most situations, the serious angler will opt for a 20-degree cone angle which provides excellent resolution and adequate bottom coverage at normal depths.

Making Necessary Adjustments

Although the various types of fishing electronics differ in the way they display information, the units are adjusted for maximum efficiency by use of the same two controls—a gain or sensitivity setting and a disturbance or suppression adjustment.

The sensitivity control usually doubles as an on-off switch. If the angler turns up the gain, he increases the unit's power to mark underwater objects. Most anglers never turn up the sensitivity high enough to read anything but the bottom. To get the most from sonar, the user must adjust the unit frequently as the boat passes from shallow water to deep water or from hard bottoms to soft bottoms.

The sensitivity or gain control should be slowly adjusted until a bottom reading appears. At that point, the gain is turned up a little more until a second echo or bottom reading appears on the dial. (The second echo should appear on the dial at twice the actual bottom depth.) When that second echo appears, the unit has been fine-tuned for sensitivity to mark everything between the transducer and the bottom, including tiny minnows, weeds, brush and, of course, walleyes.

The second adjustable control is the suppression or disturbance adjustment. Designed to eliminate electrical or physical disturbances, the suppression adjustment works much the same way as the gain control. The suppression control reduces interference when the boat is running at high speeds or when other nearby boats have units operating on the same frequency.

When suppression is turned up, the unit's sensitivity is reduced proportionally. Turning the suppression switch up too high will rob the unit of important resolution. The suppression switch should be turned off unless it's absolutely needed. When it is necessary, the suppression adjustment should be turned up just enough to suppress the troublesome interference.

Once the sonar unit is tuned properly and is working to its maximum efficiency, the angler still must be able to interpret what appears on the screen. Careful and nearly constant observation of the sonar screen can provide valuable clues concerning the mood or attitude of waiting walleyes.

For example, fish marks that are located tight to the bottom often indicate negative or neutral-minded fish that most likely will require a slow and precise presentation to tempt into biting. Fish marks a foot or more off the bottom are most likely actively feeding fish that can be caught with faster-moving presentations.

Unfortunately, no sonar unit can identify the species of fish it is marking. The angler must catch one of the fish being marked in order to know the species; however, an educated guess can usually be made based on the manner in which the fish are relating to the bottom, the size of the marks and the angler's general knowledge of species present in that body of water.

With so many brands and types of fishing sonar on the market, how can average fishermen select units that are best for their styles of fishing? Of the four basic types of fishing sonar, paper graphs, videos and liquid crystal graphs are easier to interpret than are flashers. A flasher in the hands of an angler who knows how to read the unit is a powerful fishing tool. Unfortunately, few anglers can read anything beyond depth on these units.

Flashers Faster Than Other Units

Those who have fished walleyes for years swear by flashers, stating that a flasher is the only form of fishing electronics that will mark fish when the boat is moving at high speeds. Experienced walleye hunters like Bob Propst and Gary Roach keep their eyes glued to the flasher while cruising walleye waters. The flasher records changes in bottom contour almost instantly, indicating fish on the dial with a fleeting band of light. To the untrained eye, these light bleeps usually come and go without being recognized.

Liquid crystal graph units have become popular in recent years. LCG units offer unique advantages to serious anglers. Unlike a flasher that shows a fleeting bleep of light, an LCG displays the fish for several seconds while the screen is scrolling forward.

To the angler who knows his flasher, this brief band of light is like a beacon!

The flasher is an effective and valuable fishing tool, but the only way to benefit from its use is through experience and practice. Few anglers have put in enough time on the water to learn anything beyond the basics about flashers. It appears that flashers will no longer be manufactured because most anglers use LCGs, paper graphs or video units as their primary pieces of fish-marking electronics.

A paper graph provides a picture-perfect look at fish and structure beneath the boat. Most useful for deep-water (10 to 100 feet) fishing, a paper graph is standard equipment for many top walleye professionals.

Even fish that are glued belly-to-bottom will mark on a paper graph screen—a service LCG, flasher and video units simply can't provide. The better paper graphs feature 1-inch target separation and 1,000 lines of vertical resolution.

Most serious walleye anglers use the paper graph as a second or confidence sonar unit because quality graph paper is expensive. Therefore, most anglers use a flasher or other sonar unit to locate structure and just flip on the paper graph when it's time to scout productive-looking water for signs of walleyes.

If the boat is a tiller model, the paper graph is normally mounted on top of the console or near the transom. Because they are large and heavy, paper graph units should be attached with a heavy-duty, quick-release mount.

LCGs Popular Units

New LCGs are the most popular sonar units on the market because they are among the easiest units to interpret and they cost less than top-of-the-line paper and video graphs.

The better LCG units are versatile and dependable machines. One reason for the LCG's popularity is the automatic mode feature. In this mode, the graph adjusts the sensitivity and suppresses interference. It even changes bottom ranges when necessary. Although convenient, automatic modes aren't necessarily an advantage, and on some sonar units the modes hurt the walleye angler more than they help him.

Marking walleyes holding tight to cover or structure is a difficult job for any sonar unit. Sensitivity must be set to an optimum level and suppression must be kept to a minimum. Many LCG units don't meet these standards when in the automatic mode.

If your LCG unit has a manual mode, use it. In the manual mode, sensitivity, grayline and suppression can be fine-tuned to provide the best possible underwater picture. Like a flasher, an LCG unit can be set easily to provide maximum sensitivity; however, consult the owner's manual when operating LCG units that don't have the automatic mode.

LCG units also offer loran or GPS navigational systems as built-in features. With an LCG sonar unit, anglers can find fish, navigate the boat and return to previously located hotspots.

Video graphs are the most expensive sonar devices. Many of the better video graphs provide acceptable detail (approximately 250 lines vertical resolution)—but at a staggering cost. Also, most video units are bulky and difficult to mount in a fishing boat. A third concern is their display screens. Many of these products are difficult or impossible to read in bright light.

7

GPS Technology

Global Positioning System advancements are changing the way serious anglers fish. Absolutely the biggest news to hit the fishing and marine industry since the Lowrance family introduced sonar in the 1950s, GPS satellite navigational technology is pushing sportfishing into a new dimension.

Admittedly, the notion of using radio waves broadcast from space to navigate boats on planet Earth reads like a Star Trek script. The GPS technology pioneered and developed by Rockwell International is 21st century material all right, but Captain Kirk never had it so good.

While GPS navigation is complex, the use of these units to locate more fish couldn't be simpler. To fully appreciate the benefits of GPS navigational systems, anglers must first understand how GPS differs from loran, and why this navigational system and fishing tool takes over where loran leaves off.

GPS Vs. Loran

Both loran and GPS accomplish similar tasks. Designed to help anglers navigate between destinations and return to specific fishing spots, GPS units provide a higher degree of navigational accuracy and better dependability than does the loran system.

Loran, which is widely used by sport anglers, operates off radio waves transmitted from ground-based transmitters. Developed and built during World War II, loran transmission towers are con-

Even though the idea of an instrument obtaining information from space seems complex, GPS units are easy to learn and use. This angler is using his GPS unit to navigate to his favorite walleye hotspot. (Note the small GPS antenna compared to the loran antenna.)

GPS Technology

centrated near major shipping routes throughout the country.

Anglers who live near the Atlantic, Pacific or Gulf coasts, the Great Lakes or major river systems benefit most from loran systems. Those who live and fish outside these major shipping routes may discover that loran signals are too weak to provide dependable navigational information.

More loran stations are being added every year. Unfortunately, some areas of the United States and Canada still remain uncovered by signals strong enough to benefit anglers.

Traditional loran systems consist of three to five transmitter stations. Known as a "chain," these stations include a master station and two or more secondary stations that are synchronized with the master so that both the master and the secondary stations transmit at exactly the same precise time intervals. This time interval is called the Group Repetition Interval, or GRI.

Because the distance between transmitters varies, there will be a difference in the amount of time it takes the signals from each station to reach the loran receiver. Measuring the time difference between master and secondary stations in microseconds, the loran unit plots the difference on a chart, providing an imaginary line of position with the master station and one of the secondaries. The loran receiver then measures the time difference between the master and another secondary transmitter. The point at which the two lines of position intersect is the boat's current position. Each chain has a different GRI so a different loran grid is used. (For example, anglers who fish the Great Lakes region typically operate off the 8970 GRI.)

In comparison, GPS navigational systems operate off radio waves collected simultaneously from five U.S. Department of Defense satellites orbiting the Earth. A total of 24 transmission satellites are used so that, unlike loran signals, GPS transmissions are not affected by weather fronts or storms and can be picked up anywhere on the planet.

GPS technology is a highly sophisticated navigational system which is used by both the military and the private sector. The same system used to guide missiles toward enemy targets is becoming a commercial and recreational product. When GPS is applied to fishing, anglers can actually retrace their paths on water with accuracy never before envisioned.

Sonar units equipped with GPS, however, provide anglers

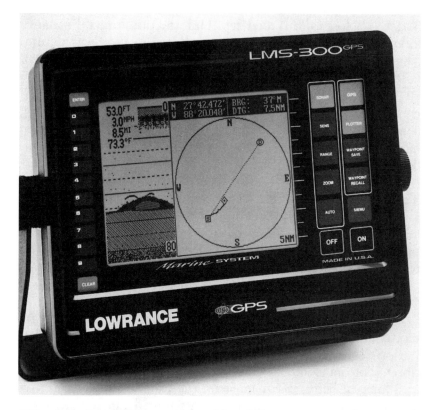

GPS units are the most modern, accurate and dependable marine navigational systems available. Useful for navigating to distant destinations or for returning to a precise fishing hotspot, GPS units represent state-of-the-art technology in marine electronics.

with much more than precise navigational data. By adding a graphics plotter, GPS units can draw detailed maps of important bottom features and contours while the angler continues fishing. It adds another dimension to sportfishing.

Structure Fishing And GPS

How can the average angler using GPS technology improve his structure-fishing skills? Walleye-fishing professionals who depend on finding and patterning fish know exactly how valuable GPS technology can be to the angler.

Gary Roach, a structure-fishing expert, describes GPS as a bottom-mapping system for structure fishermen. "Visualizing depth contours and the overall shape of key fish-holding structure is one of the most important skills an angler can develop," says

Roach. "Before GPS, I used depth information from my sonar to follow contours and make a mental picture of the structure. Thanks to the new GPS/sonar units, I can actually draw a map of bottom structure while fishing."

Roach says structure fishermen need a sonar unit with a graphics plotter to fully appreciate the benefits of GPS. When selecting a GPS unit, choose one that features a plotter with a minimum radius of one-fourth mile or smaller. The smaller the plotter radius, the more accurate and detailed the plotter picture becomes.

The Plotter Radius

A plotter radius is to GPS units what pixels are to Liquid Crystal Graph units. The more pixels (dots that make up a one-dimensional picture on an LCG) the LCG unit features, the greater the resolution or ability to show important details. GPS/plotter units provide the maximum amount of detail and accuracy when a very small radius is used.

The more sophisticated GPS units feature a $1/20$-nautical-mile plotter radius. Smaller plotter radius translates into improved definition or the ability to know precisely where the boat is in relation to bottom elements.

"Imagine being able to make on-the-water fishing maps," says Roach. "With a plotter-equipped GPS unit, I can actually trace the outline of known walleye structure and isolate the most likely fish-holding spots along a contour."

Roach says locating inside turns, the sunken-point tips or other features that typically hold fish is easy with a plotter-equipped GPS unit. It's no longer necessary to set out marker buoys or concentrate on making a mental picture of the structure; the GPS unit draws a detailed and accurate map for you.

A larger plotter radius is used for general navigation. A larger plotter radius enables the angler traveling from port to a specific fishing location to easily navigate along an established bearing.

Using GPS In Shallow Water

Roach's fishing partner, Mark Martin, uses GPS technology when he is fishing shallow-water walleye structure. "Find walleyes shallow, and they're usually hungry," says Martin. "The problem is, traditional electronics can't provide much in the way of useful information in extremely shallow water."

GPS-and-sonar combination units are practical and handy machines. A single unit provides dependable sonar, a GPS navigational system and a plotter screen that allows anglers to fish precise trolling lanes or work the edges of bottom structure with extreme accuracy.

In water less than 10 feet deep the transducer cone angle is so small that only a tiny slice of the bottom is recorded by flashers, paper graphs and LCG units. The new sonar/GPS units show depth, but they also provide a horizontal perspective that helps anglers picture the relationship of the boat to bottom structure.

"I spend a lot of time fishing points and reefs that top-out in very shallow water," says Martin. "I hunt for fish by following a contour and casting ahead of the boat. When fish are contacted, I back off a short distance and cast to the spot holding fish."

Before GPS was available, Martin used a small buoy to mark productive areas and reference points. "The problem with markers is once you throw one, it's like an open invitation to every boat in the area," he says.

Martin uses the plotter feature of a GPS to trace the outline of protruding points, sunken islands, saddles, reefs and other shallow-water structure. "Once fish are contacted, I pull back and use my plot trail as a guide to direct other casts," he says. "The plot trail shows me the location of the fish and where my boat is in relation to them. With the plotter to guide me, there's no need to throw a buoy and advertise the spot to other anglers."

The Advantages Of Fishing With GPS

Practical fishing applications for GPS technology are almost limitless. Anytime an understanding of how these fish are relating to bottom structure is needed, a graph equipped with a GPS/plotter can mean the difference between catching only a few fish or the whole school!

Walleye pros Gary Parsons and Keith Kavajecz are believed by many to be the leading authorities on trolling for walleyes. "We enjoy all facets of trolling," says Parsons, "but pulling crankbaits along winding bottom contours is one of the most challenging forms of structure fishing."

For successful structure trolling, the angler must meticulously follow bottom contours. It can be extremely difficult to isolate those bottom features that are actually holding fish.

"A complicated piece of bottom structure, such as a reef or jagged shoreline, can feature six sunken points, spines, inside turns, rock piles or other features that concentrate fish," says Kavajecz. "The angler's job is to locate these spots-on-the-spot and then concentrate his efforts on the high-percentage features."

GPS units are a tremendous aid in structure-trolling crank-baits. "The first move when I'm faced with any form of compli-cated bottom structure is to pick a contour (usually the first major drop-off) and follow that depth level around the reef, island or sunken point to be fished," says Kavajecz. "If the reef is a large one, bite off a chunk small enough to work with."

As Parsons and Kavajecz work their way around the bottom structure, the use of the depthfinder portion of their sonar/GPS unit showing depth changes helps them keep their boat posi-tioned on a specific contour. Meanwhile, by incorporating a split-image feature, they can use the plotter screen to trace a course around the reef while drawing a map that shows the reef's exact shape and any primary features (points, spines and sharp turns) associated with the structure.

"Once you've followed a contour around the structure," says Parsons, "the plot trail recorded by the GPS graphics plotter becomes a detailed road map showing the structure's shape and where the boat is in relation to important bottom features. If no fish are contacted on the first pass, position the boat deeper or shallower and use the original plot trail as a guide to fish other contours until fish are located," says Kavajecz.

Once these pros locate fish, they store the exact coordinates to the spot as a waypoint. Like loran systems, GPS units will store up to 99 waypoints for future reference. Tomorrow, a week later or next year they can return to the exact spot and pick up where they left off!

In addition to more accurate navigational data and immunity to storms and local weather fronts, GPS units feature exceptionally fast satellite lock-on. The top GPS units monitor five satellite channels. In most cases, the system is locked-on and ready for operation in less than 30 seconds.

=8=

Ever-Changing Rod And Reel Designs

S peaking from the next aisle in the sporting goods shop, a customer asked, "Can you help me pick out a good rod-and-reel combination for walleye fishing?" The clerk answered that he could, but first he needed to know what kind of walleye fishing the customer was planning. Caught by surprise, the customer didn't know how to respond to the clerk's request. After a moment of silence, he stuttered out the answer: "Uh, I'm heading to Canada in June, and, uh, I'm fishing with some work buddies."

"That's great," responded the clerk. "You'll probably be fishing a lot of jigs and rigs."

"Yah, the outfitter did tell us to bring along plenty of lead-heads, Lindy Rigs and nightcrawlers," responded the customer. "I also hear they get some nice fish trolling crankbaits in the shallows near dark."

"Sounds to me like you're in the market for a couple different rod-and-reel combinations, sir," said the clerk. "Let me show you what I've got in stock."

Similar conversations between anglers and sales clerks take place thousands of times every weekend across walleye wonderland. Choosing the right rod-and-reel combinations is no easy task for the serious walleye angler.

Successful walleye anglers understand that for every fishing presentation there's an appropriate rod-and-reel combination. The leading walleye-fishing professionals use several different

An example of the three common rod-and-reel combinations used in walleye fishing are shown here: spinning (left), baitcasting (middle) and line-counter (right).

Ever-Changing Rod And Reel Designs

rod-and-reel combinations. Not unlike bass fishing rods, walleye wands have become presentation-specific. Depending upon the presentation—jigging, rigging, slip bobbering, crankbaiting or bottom bouncing—there are up to six different rod-and-reel combinations.

No single combination will handle all the necessary walleye-fishing presentations. The pitch for presentation-specific rods seems like a sales ploy; however, it's important to remember that rods and reels are simply fishing tools. Although a carpenter can pound nails with a tack driver, he will make the job much easier for himself by using a framing hammer.

Rods—Graphite Or Fiberglass?

Since the introduction of graphite-fiber fishing rods in the 1970s, the direction of the tackle industry has been clear. The move toward lighter and more sensitive rod-building materials, such as graphite and boron, dominates the fishing scene.

Sensitivity has been the "buzz word" in the rod-building business for many years. Obviously, it's important that a rod provide its user with the ability to feel light bites (sensitivity). However, few anglers understand what makes a rod sensitive.

The material from which a rod is made influences sensitivity, but other important factors are stiffness and overall weight. The stiffer and lighter a rod, the better it will telegraph vibrations into the angler's hands.

Although few anglers realize it, a stiff action fiberglass rod may be more sensitive than a soft action graphite rod. Because a soft action rod inherently acts as a shock absorber, it robs the angler of his necessary "feel" for what's happening below.

Graphite is lighter pound for pound than fiberglass. By reducing the overall weight of the rod, the sensation of "feel" is improved. The ultimate in sensitivity is achieved when a lightweight graphite rod with a stiff action is produced.

However, not every walleye-fishing presentation requires a graphite rod's ultimate sensitivity. In fact, rod sensitivity is a minor concern for some types of fishing situations, such as when trolling with planer boards or drifting. Action, durability and overall cost are more important.

More sensitive rods are needed for jigging, rigging or structure trolling. For presentations in which "feel" is not so important

Spinning reels, such as this Daiwa model, are the most popular fishing reels among walleye enthusiasts. When jigging, slip-sinker rigging and fishing slip floats, spinning tackle is best.

(downrigger fishing, planer-boarding, drifting and slip-bobbering), rods made from less expensive fiberglass or fiberglass/graphite composites are more affordable, durable and functional.

Reels, Reels And More Reels

As confusing as rod choices can become, selection of the right walleye-fishing reels remains fairly easy. Spinning and baitcasting reels will serve all the walleye fisherman's needs.

Spinning reels are the best choice when fishing presentations that require light line and a delicate touch. Spinning reels are good choices for jigging, rigging and slip-bobber fishing.

A small- to medium-sized reel which can hold 100 yards of 6- to 8-pound-test line is ideal. A good spinning reel can range in price from $25 to $100. The more expensive models provide more

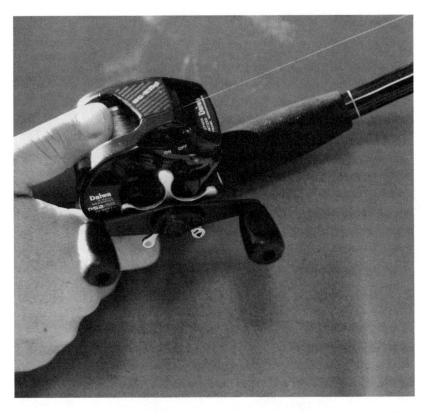

Baitcasting reels are often thought of as bass-fishing tackle. However, many walleye-fishing methods require baitcasting gear. Fishing bottom bouncers and trolling crankbaits are two walleye-fishing presentations that require the use of baitcasting tackle.

features, smoother operation and greater dependability.

Baitcasting reels are more expensive on the average than spinning reels. Ranging in price from $45 to $100, baitcasting reels have more line capacity and power to fight strong fish.

Heavy-duty fishing—such as trolling with planer boards and downriggers and fishing bottom bouncers—requires baitcasting tackle. Baitcasting reels featuring digital line counters are helpful for monitoring trolling leads.

Line-counter reels work best when trolling crankbaits with planer boards or fishing spoons and body baits off downriggers. Line-counter reels are expensive, but they're worth it.

Jigging Rods And Spinning Tackle

Personal preference enters into the purchase of jigging rods

Specialty reels, such as the line counter, are popular with anglers who troll crankbaits. The ability to quickly and easily monitor trolling leads is important when fishing crankbaits.

more than any other walleye-fishing, rod-and-reel combination. Almost every walleye fisherman uses a jig at one time or another; therefore, jigging rods are a popular subject.

Even authorities on jigging for walleyes don't agree. If the professionals can't agree, it's understandable that confusion exists among NAFC Members.

How a jig is fished determines, in part, which rod is best suited for that presentation. While there are exceptions, spinning tackle is the most widely used rod-and-reel combination for jigging.

Rods of different lengths and action are used, depending, of course, upon the type of fishing presentation—casting, vertical jigging, dragging.

Jig casting requires a rod that has enough tip action for accurately tossing light jigs. However, the rod also must be fast-handling, lightweight and highly sensitive.

A good rod for casting jigs ranges from 5 to 6 feet in length with medium action. If the rod is too stiff, casting accuracy suffers; strike detection will be difficult if the rod is too soft.

Vertical jigging is a precise form of fishing that requires ultimate sensitivity. A stiff action rod will telegraph the slightest touch better than spongy-light or medium-light action rods.

Many anglers make their vertical jigging rods stiffer by cutting a few inches off the tip of favorite medium or medium-light action rods. Cut the rodtip off cleanly with a sharp knife or fine-tooth cutting tool such as a scroll saw. Then, glue a new rodtip into place with dependable, rod-builders' cement.

Dragging jigs along the bottom calls for a softer and more forgiving rod action. A jig being dragged is likely to be dropped by a walleye the instant it feels any resistance. Therefore, a fish is less likely to drop the bait from a rod that bends easily.

Unfortunately, an angler loses some degree of sensitivity when he uses soft action rods. Therefore, anglers who fish with medium-light or light action rods often depend upon watching their line and rodtip carefully for signs of a bite, rather than relying on feel.

Rigging/Slip-Bobbering

A good rod for slip-sinker rigs doubles as an excellent slip-bobber rod. Both presentations work better with a slightly longer spinning rod, but for different reasons.

Extra rod length enables the angler to gain an advantage on the hookset during rigging. The walleye rigger must use a rod that's long enough to gobble up any and all slack when the hook is finally set.

Snapping the weight up off the bottom and pulling all the stretch out of monofilament line works best with a spinning rod that is 6 feet, 6 inches long. Shorter rods make it more difficult to set the hook effectively; longer rods are clumsy. Most anglers prefer a medium or medium-light action rod when they are live-bait rigging with slip-sinker rigs or a simple split shot and hook.

Slip-bobber fishing is another perfect presentation for the 6-foot, 6-inch to 7-foot spinning rod. Longer rods work best with bobbers because the angler can make long, delicate casts that don't tear the bait off the hook. As with slip-sinker rigging, the longer rod length also helps to pick up slack line during hooksetting.

Spinning tackle is most often used when jigging, rigging and fishing slip bobbers. Depending upon your specific presentation, rod length and action may vary.

Bottom Bouncer/Structure Trolling

The rough-and-tumble forms of walleye fishing, such as pulling bottom bouncers or trolling crankbaits, requires dependable baitcasting tackle. While many anglers are reluctant to use baitcasting equipment, the advantages this tackle brings to trolling and drift-fishing situations far outweigh the added expense.

Baitcasting tackle provides the angler with the power to land fish. Stronger drag systems, more torque to reel in fish, larger line capacity and reduced line-twist problems are just a few of the advantages that baitcasting tackle offers.

A levelwind or baitcasting reel matched with a 6-foot, 6-inch or 7-foot trigger stick is the ideal combination for pulling bottom bouncers and structure trolling. For running bottom bouncers, a medium or medium-light action rod provides the right sensitivity and flexibility. Select a rod with enough backbone to handle 3-ounce bottom bouncers for power trolling applications.

Structure trolling requires a slightly stiffer action rod. The structure troller must be able to feel his lure vibrate and wobble in the water. Medium or medium-heavy action trigger sticks work best for structure trolling a fish-by-feel technique.

Some anglers even select heavy action rods such as those used to pitch or flip for bass. A stiff trigger stick is amazingly sensitive and literally "talks" to the angler. Lure vibrations and slight takes from walleyes are telegraphed into the angler's hands.

Fast and powerful hooksets are another advantage of stiff action rods. Because these sticks have little flexibility, the angler can apply the added pressure needed to embed large treble hooks solidly.

Stiff rods can, however, create a problem. Because the rod has little shock-absorbing capability, walleyes can easily tear free of the hook if the angler pressures the fish too much at the wrong moment.

A light drag will help reduce the odds of losing fish, but back-reeling the fish may be an even better option. By putting the reel's anti-reverse switch in the "off" position, the angler can reel backward and feed line to the fish as it runs.

A technique used by most top walleye pros, backreeling is the best possible insurance against losing a fighting fish on medium-heavy or heavy action tackle.

Downrigging/Planer Boards

Some walleye-fishing presentations do not require highly sensitive and expensive graphite rods. Graphite rods aren't necessary when fishing with downriggers and planer boards. In fact, these expensive rods are the worst possible choices.

Lightweight and sensitive, graphite rods are also somewhat fragile. The torture the rods face when used for fishing 'riggers and boards would quickly ruin a set of graphite rods.

Durable fiberglass and glass/graphite composite rods work better. Rods designed for downrigger and planer-board fishing are flexible enough to absorb the shock of this kind of fishing.

The same downrigger rods used for salmon and trout will work well for walleye, too. A 7-foot to 8-foot, 6-inch rod rated to handle 10- to 20-pound-test monofilament line is about right. As in

When pulling bottom bouncers and spinners or structure trolling crankbaits, baitcasting tackle works best. Its ability to land fish is worth the slightly higher price.

fishing bottom bouncers and structure trolling, baitcasting tackle is preferred in trolling situations.

A downrigger rod must have the strength to withstand being bent over double much of the time, plus enough tip action so that light-striking walleyes can be detected.

A good planer-board rod features many of the same characteristics of a downrigger rod. Most anglers prefer a 7- to 8-foot rod when fishing from planer boards. If in-line boards are used, a medium action rod must be strong enough to handle the weight and drag of the board in the water.

Those anglers who fish with catamaran or double-board skis will find that a medium-light or even light action rod makes the fight more sporty.

Because downrigger and planer-board rod handles take a pounding, rods with foam handles are recommended because they last longer than those with cork.

Specialty Rods

Not every walleye-fishing situation falls neatly into a defined category. A few off-the-wall fishing presentations require rods and reels that are uniquely different from traditional walleye-fishing equipment.

The concept of fishing a "dead" rod got its start years ago, but only recently has dead-rod fishing caught on with walleye anglers. The father of competitive walleye fishing, Bob Propst, deserves credit for popularizing long, flexible rods for walleyes.

Dead rods get their name from the way in which they're used. Usually rigged with a small jig, slip-sinker rig or simply a split shot and hook, a dead rod is placed in a convenient rod holder while the angler concentrates on fishing a second rod.

Where it's legal, a dead rod allows the angler to keep two lines in the water and not have both of his hands tied up. "It allows me to fish two different presentations at once," says Propst. "If I'm casting a jig-and-minnow combination with one rod, I'll throw out a split shot and hook tipped with a 'crawler on a dead rod and simply drag that bait along while I'm jigging. Using this system I can experiment more with live baits, determine what type of presentation the fish are looking for and catch a lot more fish than the fella who fishes just one rod."

The ideal dead rod is long and flexible. "A good dead rod ranges from 8 to 10 feet long," says Propst. "I like a spinning-style rod with a soft action that bends easily when a fish picks up the bait. Because you're not actually holding this rod in your hand, the reaction time in setting the hook is slower. A soft action rod gives the angler a few precious extra seconds to set the hook before the fish feels resistance and drops the bait."

A fishing technique known as dibbling is also becoming popular where anglers are faced with walleyes that rest and feed in dense weed patches. Like crappie fishermen who use long cane poles to reach out away from the boat, dibbling involves using a long, stiff rod to vertical jig in dense weed patches.

A bass flippin' stick is the ideal rod for this type of fishing. When a fish is hooked, the flippin' stick's heavy action helps the angler quickly pull the fish out of heavy cover.

Monofilament And Rod/Reel Combinations

The most balanced rod-and-reel combination is useless without good monofilament line. There are numerous line sizes and types that will best meet the angler's specific needs in every type of fishing presentation.

The dibbling technique has become an effective way to catch walleyes in thick weed patches. This angler is vertical jigging with a bass flippin' stick, one of the best rods for this fishing situation.

Ever-Changing Rod And Reel Designs

Monofilament can be described as coming in three basic flavors: limp-casting lines, abrasion-resistant trolling lines and copolymer lines.

Limp lines are the best choice when the angler must cast his lure or bait a considerable distance, and when small lures and a delicate touch are needed. For all practical purposes, limp fishing lines usually fall in the 4-, 6- and 8-pound test category because lighter lines are rarely needed. However, when the situation requires heavier line, a more abrasion-resistant trolling line will work best.

Spinning tackle and limp-casting line form a perfect match for such popular walleye-fishing presentations as casting jigs, vertical jigging, slip-sinker rigging and fishing slip bobbers. Used with the correct rod-and-reel combination, limp-casting lines are ideal for casting and giving action to small lures.

Heavy-duty fishing situations, such as trolling crankbaits with planer boards, dragging bottom bouncers armed with spinners and fishing jigging spoons, requires tough fishing line. A durable outer coating protects the line from being damaged on wood, weeds, rocks or other objects in the water.

Because they are stiffer than casting lines, abrasion-resistant lines aren't suitable for delicate situations. Line weights ranging from 10- to 20-pound test are widely used in walleye fishing.

Lines of 10-, 12- and 14-pound test are by far the most popular; they are best matched with levelwind reels and baitcasting tackle. An excellent line for trolling, the abrasion-resistant monofilament is also ideal for terminal tackle such as 'crawler harnesses, slip-sinker snells and other live-bait rigs.

A third form of monofilament has become very popular in recent years. A copolymer line is thinner than regular monofilament, flexible, tough and has very little stretch. Hailed as super lines, copolymer fishing lines have some major advantages and a few shortcomings. Although most copolymer fishing lines perform well when they're new, the high-tech lines seem to deteriorate faster than traditional nylon monofilament.

For best results, change copolymer lines frequently, and retie and test lures often, too. The low-stretch characteristic of these lines also means that drag settings must be constantly checked and rechecked so that a large fish can't overstress the line.

Finally, even a slight nick will cause a copolymer line to lose

Complete Angler's Library

most of its strength. Because these lines have little stretch, the slightest nick can quickly lead to a line break.

Check all monofilament line for damage and replace the line often. Monofilament is the cheapest part of any fishing trip. Don't let the cost of a spool of monofilament cost you a nice fish.

Summing It Up

No single rod-and-reel combination is ideal for all types of walleye fishing. Fishing for marble eyes has become too sophisticated and complicated for that. The angler who takes walleye fishing seriously is likely to have six or more combinations that meet specific needs. Those who try to get by with less may be missing an important part of the sport of walleye fishing. After all, keeping up with the trends is half the fun.

9

Terminal Tackle Trends

Anglers constantly look for shortcuts. A new lure or product that promises to improve an angler's fish-catching ability is sure to attract attention. It would be great if every fishing lure on the market was a good product. Unfortunately, that's not the case; however, who is to say that one lure is good and another is bad?

Let the buyer beware. Tackle shops are full of lures that end up dusty, marked down and stored in the bargain bin. Rarely do new lures become popular, productive and long-standing walleye-fishing tools.

"Fishing lures go through cycles," says Larry Gorske, a Michigan fishing-tackle retailer. "A new lure is likely to sell well for a couple of seasons before interest in the bait and sales drop off. Because lures don't suddenly stop producing fish, it's safe to say the anglers who purchase them are probably as fickle as the fish."

Many factors influence the purchase of fishing lures. Word of mouth from anglers, suggestions from tackle retailers, recommendations in magazine articles and advertising claims all help sell terminal tackle.

Endorsements from popular professional anglers or television celebrities have a dramatic impact on fishing-tackle sales in this country. "When Ken Cook won the B.A.S.S. Masters Classic, the lures he used became hot items instantly," explains Gorske. "Baits that had been collecting dust on my shelves for years were suddenly converted into hot selling items.

When purchasing walleye-fishing tackle, select high-quality items that have been proven successful. Certain brands become popular because the manufacturer consistently produces high-quality items. These anglers teamed up to land a walleye that hit a brightly colored jig.

Terminal Tackle Trends

"Walleye anglers are just as vulnerable to tackle trends as bass anglers," says Gorske. "When Gary Parsons and Keith Kavajecz won the Masters Walleye Circuit World Championship on jigging spoons, every walleye fisherman and his brother added a few of these lures to his collection. Once the dust settled, sales of jigging spoons returned to normal."

Despite pro-angler endorsements, advertising claims and testimonials, a surprisingly small selection of walleye-fishing lures produces the vast majority of the fish taken each year. For a modest investment, anglers can fill their tackle-box trays with lures that have survived the test of time.

That's not to say that new lures aren't worth checking out. Occasionally, products that make fishing a more productive and enjoyable experience are introduced. However, glancing into the tackle box of a knowledgeable fisherman usually tells the story. For walleye fishing, it's difficult to improve upon live bait. Fishing lures designed to present minnows, nightcrawlers or leeches produce the most walleyes. A basic assortment of jigs, live-bait rigs, spinners and slip-bobber systems will serve the beginner, weekend warrior and professional angler equally well.

Live bait isn't the only way to catch walleyes, but starting with classic lures that have produced walleyes for generations makes sense. Putting together a solid assortment of leadhead jigs is an ideal place to start.

Like most fishing lures, jigs come in various sizes, shapes and colors. Nothing more than an Aberdeen-style hook with a chunk of lead molded in place, jigs serve a basic function of keeping the bait on or near the bottom. Obviously, different sizes, or weights, of jigs are necessary to properly fish different depths.

The most common jig sizes used by walleye anglers are ¹⁄₁₆, ⅛, ¼ and ⅜ ounce. Of these five sizes, the ⅛- and ¼-ounce versions are the workhorses. In exceptionally shallow situations, the ¹⁄₁₆ is important; in deep water, the ⅜-ounce jig works best.

Determining which size jig to use isn't difficult—use just enough weight to keep the bait on bottom.

Jig-head designs also make a difference. Certain shaped jig heads work better with certain presentations. For example, fishing in weeds clearly calls for a jig that slides through vegetation with the least amount of hang-ups. When fishing weeds, anglers should select jigs with the hook eye protruding straight out of the

A surprisingly small assortment of tackle will catch walleyes in most situations. Anglers should stock up on the basics, including jigs, rigs, slip bobbers, bottom bouncers and crankbaits. Fads in the tackle business come and go, but the basics are here to stay.

front of the lure. Positioning the hook eye in the front allows these jigs to slip through aquatic growth so that pieces of weeds or other debris don't collect at the point where the line connects to the jig.

On standard roundheaded jigs, the hook eye comes out of the top of the lure. This type of jig works best when fished in a vertical or near vertical position.

Flattened, or stand-up-style jig heads also have their place. Designed so that the bait is positioned upward when resting on the bottom, stand-up jigs make the bait more visible to fish and more snag-resistant when they are slowly dragged along the bottom. Many different versions of stand-up jigs exist, but all do basically the same thing.

Action-style jig heads fall into another category. Jigs with flipper blades, spinners or propellers are becoming more popular every year. The added flash and slower drop rate that these jigs offer can dramatically improve catching success in many different jigging situations.

Snag-free jig heads are also useful when leadheads are fished in submerged timber. Most of these jigs feature some sort of plastic or wire weed guard that helps prevent the hook point from snagging.

All these common jig-head designs should have a place in the walleye fisherman's tackle box. A good assortment of leadheads wouldn't be complete, however, without a few plastic grub bodies. Dressing a jig with a plastic body adds action, color and bulk to the presentation. Plastic tails come in many shapes and sizes. Twister or swirl-tail grubs, shad-style bodies and tube baits are among the most popular plastic jig dressings.

If the leadhead jig is the No. 1 walleye lure, then live-bait rigs are No. 2. The famous Lindy Rig developed by the Lindner brothers has become legendary for its fish-catching ability. Many manufacturers offer prepackaged live-bait rigs designed especially for walleye fishing.

Despite the convenience of pretied rigs, some anglers prefer to purchase components separately and use their own line to tie live-bait rigs as needed. The basic components of a live-bait rig include slip-type or walking sinkers, small barrel swivels and different hook styles and sizes to accommodate minnows, leeches and nightcrawlers.

A few sinkers in weights ranging from ⅛ to ½ ounce will handle most walleye-fishing situations. Barrel swivels stop the sinker from sliding down to the bait. These swivels also make a convenient attachment point to add different length leaders. Hooks ranging from large Aberdeens to small beak styles are used on live-bait rigs. The size and style of hook depends upon the size and type of live bait.

Rigging with chubs, suckers or other large minnows calls for using No. 1 or 2 Aberdeen hooks. The wide gap between the shank and the hook point helps increase hooking ratios.

Smaller minnows are often fished on a No. 2 beak-style hook. The same hook in No. 4 or 6 is popular when fishing with 'crawlers and leeches.

The standard live-bait rig will be popular as long as walleye fillets taste good, but quick-change rigs offering the option to change sinker weights are becoming very popular.

Convenient and easy to use, these rigs feature a plastic clip that slides on the line and accepts a walking-style sinker. If a different weight is desired, the angler simply clips a new weight in place without having to cut or tie the rig.

Live-bait rigs are traditionally fished with an 18- to 24-inch leader connected to a single hook. Longer leader lengths averaging 36 to 60 inches are starting to take over the show. Long-leader rigs are often referred to as finesse rigs. Lengthening the leader adds a little more action to bait rigs and further separates the bait from the rigging weight. When fishing is tough, long leaders often trigger strikes when leads of traditional length fail.

Snelled spinners, floating jig heads and other attractors are also used with slip-sinker rigs. The garden variety nightcrawler harness of yesterday has been largely replaced with longer harnesses made with light line, and high-quality hooks.

Known simply as walleye spinners, these modern-day versions of the worm harness are available with every blade style, color combination and hook arrangement imaginable. Colorado- and Indiana-style blades remain popular, but willow-leaf and French-style blades and prop-like propellers also take walleyes.

A 36- to 60-inch spinner is considered normal today, but a few years ago purchasing a spinner rig this long would have been impossible. Nightcrawler harnesses are normally tied with two beak-style hooks. Minnow and leech spinners sprouting a single Aberdeen or beak-style hook are also available.

A relatively new type of live-bait sinker designed to keep spinner rigs running smoothly over rock- and snag-filled bottoms has stolen the bait-rigging scene in recent years.

The Missouri River bottom-bouncer sinker doesn't look like much, but this simple wire and lead contraption may soon surpass all other versions of live-bait rigging systems in sales. Designed to slide over the bottom while presenting the bait at the walleye's eye level, these weights follow rapidly changing contours better than slip sinkers and other weights.

An ideal sinker for slow trolling or drifting spinner rigs, plain hook and leader live-bait snells and even shallow-diving crankbaits can be used in combination with bottom bouncers. Bottom bouncers shouldn't be considered a replacement for the slip-sinker rig. Sand, clay or gravel bottoms that contain few potential snags are the ideal environment for slip-sinker rigging. Bottom bouncers shine when trolled at higher speeds or when used in areas that contain broken rock, brush and other debris that devour traditional bait rigs.

Most bouncers are a 12- to 14-inch-long chunk of wire with a lead weight molded in place midway on the shaft. A short wire arm with a snap swivel accepts various leader and live-bait combinations.

When dragged along the bottom, bouncers work their way along in a rocking motion that imparts a stop-and-flutter action to the attached bait rig. This added action makes bouncers a deadly rigging option.

The latest rigging craze combines the best features of slip-sinker rigs and bottom bouncers. Slip-sinker rigs feed a fish slack line once a bite is detected, but bouncers are more snag-resistant.

The latest in bottom bouncers is a single-arm wire bouncer rigged to slide on the line like a walking-style sinker. The same quick-change sinker snap popular with slip-sinker riggers readily accepts these single-arm bottom bouncers.

When dragged at approximately a 45-degree angle behind the boat, this rig "walks" through snags and positions the bait a few inches off the bottom. When a strike is detected, the angler feeds the fish slack line for a few seconds before setting the hook.

Seeming to be the best of both worlds, these bouncers are catching on fast. Other bait rigs allowing the angler to easily adjust leader length are also available. It's difficult to improve upon a legendary system of catching walleyes, but many of the newest live-bait rigs appear to do just that.

Slip bobbers are an often overlooked bait-rigging option. Primarily used by anglers who usually fish natural lakes having thick weed patches or wind-swept rock reefs, a balanced slip-bobber rig catches walleyes when other rigging systems fail.

The basic slip-bobber rig consists of a bobber stop, wooden or plastic float, split shots and a hook. Small enough to reel right up through the guides, bobber stops, which come in many styles, enable an angler to set the bait depth.

Floats are also available in various sizes, shapes and materials. Cigar, pencil and oval-shaped models are the most popular among walleye fishermen.

At the terminal end, many different hooks and small jigs work well with bobbers and will hook and hold walleyes. While Aberdeen

Some of the most exciting advancements in terminal tackle have been made with crankbaits. Every year new models appear with deeper diving ranges, improved colors and better actions. Every walleye angler should have an assortment of crankbaits in his tackle box.

and beak-style hooks see a lot of bobber-rig action, the new wide-bend hooks are even better. Designed to offer excellent hooking ratios with bobber rigs, the new wide-bend hooks make it possible for an angler to select a slightly smaller-sized hook than he would normally.

No matter which bobber stop, float or hook is used, floats must be counterbalanced with split shot so that the slightest nibble will pull the float under the surface. This simple point separates the serious anglers from the weekenders—as far as float fishing is concerned.

Despite being one of the least used live-bait rigging options, slip bobbers are far from toys. Precise fishing instruments, bobber rigs in the hands of a skilled angler mean walleye success.

Classic live-bait fishing lures and rigs can take the average walleye angler a long way. However, no tackle collection would be complete without a few plastic and wood minnow imitations, collectively referred to as crankbaits or plugs.

Like other fishing lures, crankbaits are designed to imitate something a walleye would eat. An angler would need a healthy inheritance to purchase a sample of each model crankbait available. Fortunately, a huge selection of lures isn't necessary for an angler to enjoy walleye fishing success with plugs. All crankbaits fall into two basic categories: sinkers and floater/divers.

The floater/divers are the most popular with walleye anglers. Designed to float when at rest and to dive when retrieved or trolled, these lures are further categorized into shallow-, medium- and deep-diving models.

A shallow-diving crankbait will dive roughly about 1 to 6 feet beneath the surface, medium divers achieve a maximum depth of 6 to 12 feet and deep divers will dredge up walleyes from 12 to 40 feet down.

The diving lip's size, the amount of line let out and the line's diameter all influence a crankbait's depth-diving range. Every year new crankbaits in various new-and-improved fish-catching colors and models are introduced. Some are designed to dive deeper; others offer rattles or flashy finishes.

Knots And Knot Strength

No discussion of terminal tackle would be complete without a few suggestions on how monofilament line should be attached to the various fishing lures. Jigs, livebait snells and slip-bobber rigs are best attached directly to the fishing line with a sturdy knot, while the crankbaits, spoons and bottom bouncers are best attached to a durable snap that is tied to the line.

Walleye anglers use many different knots, and the best knots are those that are easy to tie and are strong. Remember that some knots reduce the break-strength of monofilament by as much as 50 percent! Binding or cutting-type knots on monofilament lines should be avoided.

The Trilene knot is simple, and one of the strongest and easiest knots to tie. Start by running the line through the lure's line tie, then bring the line through the same attachment point a second time, forming a loop. Next, wrap the loose end of the line around the main line five times. Without letting the wraps come undone, take the tag end and run it through the opening formed by the first line wrap. Carefully pull both ends of the line until the knot is tight.

Trim the Trilene knot, leaving about ⅛ inch of the tag line attached. This knot is an excellent way to attach jigs, hooks and other lures or baits to monofilament line.

The Palomar is even stronger than the Trilene knot and just as easy to tie. Double about 6 inches of line and pass the doubled end through the eye of a jig, hook or snap. Let the lure/hook hang loose and tie a loose overhand knot in the doubled line. Don't tighten up the knot yet. Instead, place the lure through the loop that was formed when the overhand knot was tied. Now pull both the tag end and the standing line together slowly. Clip the tag end within ⅛ inch of the knot.

The Palomar knot is ideal for attaching jigs, hooks and snaps to monofilament. About the only time this knot isn't useful is when you're tying large plugs directly to monofilament line.

The snell knot is also a handy knot for the walleye fisherman. Used to tie worm harnesses, slip-sinker rigging leaders and other live-bait rigs, the snell knot is the strongest of all knots.

Cut a predetermined length of monofilament line and run one end through the hook eye leaving approximately 1 inch of tag. Pinch the tag line against the hook shank with two fingers and wrap the main line around the hook shank and tag about nine times. Carefully pinch the wraps so they don't come undone, and run the end of the main line through the hook eye from the opposite direction.

Simply pull the knot tight and trim off the tag end ⅛ inch from the knot. This simple knot is strong and can be used for many fishing applications.

Remember, it's best to wet all knots before pulling them tight. Friction from dry line sliding against itself can lead to line damage. It's these little details that prevent terminal tackle from being donated to the bottom, or worse yet, to a waiting walleye.

=10=

The Science Of Hooking

Thousands of walleyes escape each year because anglers take their hooks for granted. Hooks are the most important and most overlooked aspect of fishing. Don't stop reading! This chapter isn't another lecture about the virtues of sharp hooks. Every angler worth his Aberdeens knows that sharp hooks bite better than dull ones.

Professional angler and author Mike McClelland was one of the first professional anglers to recognize and apply the science of hooking to walleye fishing. "Traditionally, walleye fishermen have always used No. 6 or No. 8 hooks that are easy to hide in the bait," says McClelland. "Hiding the hook sounds good in theory, but using small hooks to catch fish equipped with hard, bony mouths breaks all the rules of common sense."

McClelland, a leading money winner on the professional walleye circuit, clawed his way to the top by applying common sense in competition and putting the odds in his favor. "I never use a hook smaller than a No. 4 when walleye fishing," says McClelland. "I also prefer light, wire hooks that can be bent out and recovered if the hook snags."

Wire hooks will bend, allowing the hook to pull free of snags. Tempered wire used in making the hooks bends and then springs back into shape without breaking. This seemingly small feature saves many hooks and minimizes the amount of fishing time wasted by tying on new tackle.

McClelland made the switch to larger hooks in the early '70s

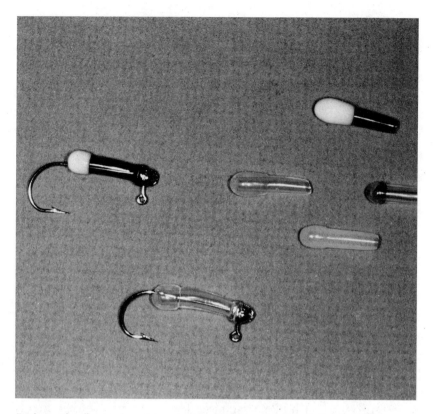

Professional walleye anglers advise using bigger hooks, such as No. 4, 2 or 1. This ¹⁄₆₄-ounce Jig-A-Whopper Bobber has a No. 2 hook. The larger hook makes it easier to reach back into the walleye's mouth, enabling the hook point to penetrate soft tissue.

when walleye tournaments were just becoming popular. "Before I fished walleyes professionally," he says, "I spent a lot of time fishing bass tournaments. Bass anglers use big hooks with long shanks and a wide gap or bite. These oversized hooks make sense because they're large enough to reach back into the softer and more easily penetrated part of the fish's mouth. It's the same with walleyes!"

McClelland's tournament success has caused thousands of anglers to reevaluate their selection of fish hooks. "Walleyes have a large, bony mouth that's resistant to hook penetration," says McClelland. "The first step toward achieving higher hooking ratios is going to larger hooks. The second step is understanding the two stages of hooking a fish."

Simply setting the hook hard doesn't guarantee you'll catch more fish. To hook more walleyes you have to stick the fish with

The Science Of Hooking   99 the hook point; however, in order to hang onto them, the hook must penetrate past the barb.

McClelland explains that there are two parts to the science of hooking. Sticking or embedding the point of the hook is only half the game. Penetrating the flesh and burying the hook past the barb prevents the walleye from shaking the hook and escaping.

"Unfortunately, many hooks only stick the fish that bite," says McClelland. "Hooks designed to offer a needle-like point stick the hard tissue inside a fish's mouth effectively, but they don't penetrate well. During the fight, the hook frequently works free, and the fish escapes. To penetrate and hold effectively, a hook must have a knife or cutting edge."

Dr. Steven Holt, a walleye tournament fisherman, explains how a hook with a cutting edge can dramatically increase the ratio of fish hooked and landed. "In medical school, I learned how to suture wounds," says Holt. "I remember being amazed how difficult it was to push a round needle through the tissue. Triangular shaped needles with knife-like edges easily sliced through the tissue and made the job of suturing simple."

Imagining the process of hooking and fighting a walleye makes it easier to understand why hooks must prick and penetrate to be effective. When a walleye feeds, it inhales the food by sucking water into its mouth like a vacuum. The moment the angler feels a bite, he rears back on his rod and sets the hook point into the fish's mouth. The second the fish realizes something is wrong, he forces water out through his mouth and shakes his head in an effort to rid himself of the foreign matter.

Meanwhile, the angler leans into the fish and puts pressure on the hook. If the hook has a sharp cutting edge, it starts to work deep into the tissue of the fish's mouth. Every time the fish shakes his head back and forth, the hook cuts deeper and quickly penetrates to the barb.

On the other hand, if the hook were one with a needle-like point, it probably pricked the hard bony surface of the fish's mouth, but wasn't able to penetrate past the barb. If this is the case, chances are good that the fish will be able to struggle until the hook is finally freed.

Leading hook manufacturers are taking the science of hooking to even greater levels. Using a specially designed computer, manufacturers have conducted tests with many different hooks to mea-

Walleye anglers have many different hooks to choose from. The new cutting-edge hooks are setting the stage for future hook development. Cutting-edge hooks penetrate up to 2.5 times easier than traditional round-point hooks.

sure the grams of force needed for point and barb penetration.

"Fish hooks featuring a knife-like or cutting edge penetrate with two-and-a-half times less force than traditional needle-point hooks," says Skip Mortensen, a major manufacturer of walleye fishing hooks. "The future of fish-hook design is definitely heading toward cutting-edge-style hooks."

Steven Holt says, "Knife-edge-style hooks are being produced by many manufacturers. Choosing the exact model and size hook for the job is important. Obviously, different walleye-fishing situations require different hooks. The type of bait to be used, the cover to be fished and the actual presentation determine the best possible hook choice."

Lindy Rigging

Rigging with live minnows, 'crawlers or leeches produces more fish dinners than just about any other walleye presentation. When choosing a hook for rigging, the type and size of bait are important considerations. The pros suggest using a No. 4 beak or Viking hook when rigging with 'crawlers or leeches. These compact hooks feature a short shank and turned up eye that's easy to hide in the bait and are ideal for use with snell knots.

Single-hook snells are used primarily when fishing leeches or minnows. If 'crawlers are used, a two-hook snell provides better hookups and fewer missed fish.

Tom Irwin, a walleye guide working out of Muskegon, Michigan, prefers a two-hook rig when fishing 'crawlers. "I tie my own 'crawler rigs using two No. 4 hooks spaced approximately 6 inches apart," says Irwin. "Hooks used with 'crawlers must be small enough so as not to interfere with the natural undulating action of a 'crawler, yet large enough to bite and hold securely. The space between the hooks is also critical."

According to Irwin, most commercially available two-hook snells have the hooks spaced only 2 to 3 inches apart. "This narrow hook placement is asking for short bites and half-eaten 'crawlers. I prefer to tie my own snells that spread out the hooks a little more than normal. The wider spacing allows the second hook to reach farther back in the 'crawler and act like a stinger hook."

If minnows are the bait of choice, a larger hook is advised. Depending upon the size of the minnow, a No. 4, 2, 1 or even 1/0 Aberdeen hook is ideal for the bony mouth of a walleye.

Aberdeen-style hooks have a slightly wider hook gap than traditional baitholder-style hooks. The soft wire these hooks are made from can also be straightened out and retrieved from snags that would claim other hooks.

Prepackaged walleye-fishing snells are popular with anglers who like to spend their spare time fishing. Prepackaged rigs help anglers match the proper hook type and size with the ideal leader length for successful walleye fishing.

Snell length for most live-bait rigging applications varies from 18 to 36 inches. In extremely clear water or if walleyes are spooky, a longer snell length of 48 to 60 inches works best.

Finding commercially tied long-leader snells and two-hook snells with a wide hook placement is difficult at best. A few manufacturers are beginning to offer "custom quality" live-bait rigs that give the angler a choice.

Slip-Bobbering Is Effective

You don't have to live on Lake Mille Lacs in Minnesota to know that slip-bobbering is one of the most effective ways to fish walleyes on shallow rock reefs and in the weeds. Choosing the

Adding a stinger hook is an excellent way to catch light-biting walleyes. Mike Norris, the author's tournament fishing partner, hefts a dandy walleye that hit a jig-and-minnow combination. If you look closely, you'll notice the jig is several inches from the fish's mouth. A No. 10 stinger hook was used.

The Science Of Hooking

proper hook can substantially increase hooking ratios. A hook style that lends itself to a vertical hookset is critical.

When fishing floats for walleyes, a No. 10 wide-gap hook is ideal. The open sprout on these hooks offers the best possible bite on vertical hooksets. Wide-bend hooks enable the angler to select a smaller hook size than normal without sacrificing hooking or holding power.

Some anglers substitute a small leadhead jig for wide-bend hooks. The jig doubles as a hook and weight to keep the bait positioned at the desired depth. A crappie-sized ($\frac{1}{32}$- or $\frac{1}{16}$-ounce) jig tipped with a lively leech or minnow has accounted for many walleyes when fished in combination with a slip float.

The best jigs for float fishing have the hook eye positioned out of the top of the leadhead. A hook eye on the top keeps the bait resting in a natural, horizontal position.

Bottom Bouncers

A bottom bouncer armed with a 4-foot leader and a single Aberdeen-style hook is a simple yet deadly walleye weapon. Unleashed on walleyes holding near deep-water structure, this live-bait rigging option delivers a high hooking percentage.

"I used a bottom bouncer and leeches to take second place during a tournament on Rainy Lake," says McClelland. "The fish were holding tight to the edges of deep-water humps. All I had to do was work my way around the edges of the structure until I marked fish, then use my electric motor to drag the bottom bouncer and leech through the school."

The bottom bouncer kept McClelland's leech on the bottom. At the business end, a single gold No. 1 Aberdeen hook stuck and held dozens of fish during the three-day tourney.

McClelland hooked and landed a high percentage of the fish that inhaled the ribbon leech. "I chose a long-shank Aberdeen because I wanted the hook to reach back into the fish's mouth," says McClelland. "The tissue in the back of a walleye's mouth is much softer and easier to penetrate with a hook than the bone and hard tissue around the jaw."

Replacing Treble Hooks On Crankbaits

Lots of anglers sharpen the treble hooks on their crankbaits, but few go the extra mile and replace those hooks that can't deliver adequate penetration. Few crankbaits come factory-armed with exactly the right size or type of hooks.

Good hooks are expensive, but anglers shouldn't be shy about replacing treble hooks on crankbaits. After all, what good is a lure if fish strike it but aren't hooked?

On deep-diving crankbaits, the back treble hook should be replaced with a round-bend-style treble hook one size larger than the hook installed at the factory. Round-bend hooks have a wider hook gap that's more likely to grab and hold.

Replacing the back hook on diving baits is the most critical because, in most cases, it's the trailing hook that deserves the credit for holding a struggling fish.

Going with a hook one size larger than normal significantly increases the lure's hooking ratios and has little effect on its diving or swimming action. Many lures come from the factory with hooks that are too small to get the job done effectively.

It's especially important to replace the hooks on fat-bodied cranks. Wide-bodied cranks are notoriously lousy hookers. When the lure's width exceeds the hook's width, a hard-mouthed fish, such as a walleye, will either be lightly hooked or won't be hooked at all.

When a walleye grabs a minnow, it bites down, using its sharp teeth to kill the prey. When a walleye strikes at a crankbait, it bites down but the hard body of the lure prevents the fish from making a normal bite. Wide-bodied cranks draw lots of strikes. Unfortunately, fish are often missed during the hookset when the lure is jerked free because its hooks rarely stick flesh.

Replacing treble hooks can be expensive, but many anglers prefer it because it makes their lures produce better. However, slightly bending the hook to open the gap on factory-installed hooks can increase hooking success without additional expense. Using a pair of needle-nosed pliers, grasp the hook below the barb and carefully bend the hook point out until the distance between the point and the shank is increased significantly. Bending hooks open increases the hook gap, much like adding larger hooks. Unfortunately, this remedy doesn't work on all hooks because some are made of brittle metal and will break.

How Sharp Is Sharp?

A fish hook simply can't be too sharp for taking walleyes.

Sharp hooks are mandatory for many fishing methods, especially crankbait trolling. A small file is still the best way to put a sticky, sharp edge on fish hooks.

Anglers try to keep an edge on their hooks in various ways—using hand-operated hones, files, stones and battery-powered hook sharpeners. Although battery-operated hook sharpeners are popular, most are designed to produce a needle-like point instead of a cutting edge. Even though hooks sharpened by an orbiting-type tool may seem sharp, they will not penetrate or hold, in most cases, as well as a hook that is carefully filed by hand.

It's hard to beat a simple flat file for sharpening fish hooks. With the hook held firmly in your hand, drag the file on a couple passes along each side of the hook. A final stroke along the front face of the hook removes any burr edge and puts a clean chisel-like cutting edge on the hook.

Always file away from your hand, and from the hook bend toward the point. Filing this way helps keep the angler from sticking himself and prevents burr edges from developing on the hook.

All three points on a treble hook should be given equal treatment. Then give it the thumbnail test. If hooks are sharpened properly, they should be sticky sharp.

Also remember that hooks must be resharpened frequently to maintain an edge. Conscientious anglers wear out their hooks long before the lures are ready to be retired. Of course, other little details like line and knot strength are important because no hook will penetrate thoroughly if the line is damaged and breaks or a knot slips during the hookset or the fight.

Most serious anglers will cut off their lures and reattach them several times during a fishing day. This tedious task can, and often does, prevent unnecessary fish break-offs.

Advancements in hook design are changing the way walleye anglers think and fish. The trend in walleye fishing is toward bigger hooks, hooks with points having cutting-style knife edges. Together these features make a first-rate fish hook.

How It's Done

=11=

Casting, Dragging And Swimming Jigs

Simplicity is the first step toward perfection. Whoever invented the common leadhead jig should be proud. Not since the metal fish hook has a simpler, more effective or versatile fishing lure hit the market. Effective on all species of freshwater game and panfish, leadheads are especially popular with walleye fishermen. Walleyes spend a considerable amount of time hugging bottom, making them prime jig-fishing targets.

Jigs can be fished anywhere in the water column from just beneath the surface to kissing the sand. However, in most jigging presentations, these lures hop, dance or drag near bottom.

Leadheads are frequently fished in combination with minnows, nightcrawlers, leeches, pork rind and a huge assortment of plastic grub bodies and action-tail baits. Adding these baits or attractors changes the lure's look, feel, taste and action.

Jig-Head Shapes And Features

A generous assortment of leadheads is likely to be found in every walleye boat. Leadhead jigs are available in various shapes, sizes and colors. To the casual observer, one jig may appear pretty much the same as the next. Closer examination reveals that jigs, like many other fishing lures, are designed for specific fishing presentations. Some models have hook guards, making them snag-resistant in weeds, timber or other snag-producing areas. Some feature specially shaped head designs, and still others incorporate

This angler knows that jigging produces walleyes when other faster presentations fail. If limited to only one fishing lure, most serious anglers would use the leadhead jig.

Casting, Dragging And Swimming Jigs

spinner blades or other types of attractors.

The shape and/or features of a jig often make a big difference in how the lure performs under different angling situations. Obviously, fishing jigs among submerged trees or brush is going to result in a lot of lost lures unless a snag-resistant model is used.

Fishing jigs in thick aquatic weeds requires a specially designed head shape that will find its way through heavy cover with few hang-ups and hassles. Still other jig-head shapes are helpful when the lure must be dragged slowly along the bottom in order to produce strikes. Understanding how to recognize these fishing situations and selecting the correct tool for the job separates good jig-fishermen from those anglers who catch only a few fish while jigging.

Jig-head shapes seem to have no limit. Despite subtle differences in head configuration, most jigs fall neatly into three categories: round-head, stand-up and weedless.

The head portion's shape of the round-head jig is round or ball-like. The most common and versatile of all leadhead designs, round-head walleye jigs are available in sizes ranging from 1/16 ounce to a full ounce or more. The most common weights are 1/8, 1/4 and 3/8 ounce.

Stand-up jig heads are designed to stand upright at rest, positioning the bait slightly off bottom where fish are more likely to see it. Many manufacturers have developed stand-up jig models that work well.

Stand-up jigs are most effective when the angler is slowly dragging the lure along bottom. While the jig is being slowly dragged along bottom, the head design keeps the hook from snagging and the bait in clear view of nearby fish.

Dragging jigs can be a deadly presentation on a snag-free bottom. Mud, clay, gravel or sand flats are prime locations to drag jigs. Areas that feature rocky bottoms, riprap, submerged timber or heavy weed growth are best fished with other presentations and jig-head designs.

Many different models of weedless jigs are designed to fish these snag-filled areas. Some weedless jigs feature plastic or wire brush guards that prevent the jig hook from easily catching on debris. Other jig-head styles depend primarily on shape and eye placement to make them snag-resistant.

The ideal jig for fishing in submerged timber or brush has a

Leadhead jigs come in many different sizes, shapes and colors. Despite their physical appearances, all jigs fall into three basic categories: round-head, stand-up and weedless. All three groups have specific functions.

plastic or wire guard mounted into the jig's head that extends beyond the hook point. The brush guard protects the hook point, allowing the jig to be fished through snag-filled waters with very few hang-ups. When a walleye inhales the jig into its mouth, the guard collapses enough to allow hook-point penetration.

Catching fish with jigs having brush or weed guards requires a solid hookset. It takes a little extra pressure to flatten the brush guard and drive the hook home with authority.

Using a jigging rod with a little stiffer action than normal is a good idea when you're fishing weedless-style jigs. The added backbone this rod contains ensures a solid hookset and better hook penetration. A stiff action rod is also useful for wrestling a struggling fish away from potential snags.

Jigs designed for fishing in weeds feature a streamlined shape and an eye that extends from the front of the lure. Most jigs have an eye that protrudes out of the top of the jig head. These are fine for casting or dragging in most situations, but they don't work well for fishing in weeds. That's because the angle formed between the point where the line attaches to the jig and the front of the lure has a tendency to pick up pieces of weeds or other debris.

Casting, Dragging And Swimming Jigs

Jig-Head Styles

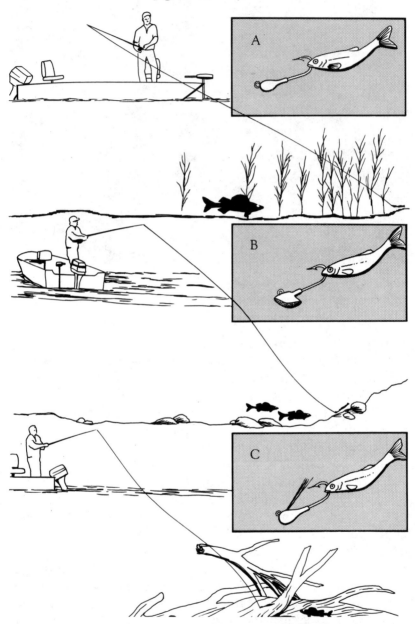

Good weed jigs (A) should have the eye coming out of the front of the lure. This enables the lure to pull through weeds and other debris with few hangups. Stand-up jigs (B) are ideal for dragging along the bottom; they position the bait off the bottom. Weedless jigs (C) are tailor-made for fishing in heavy cover, such as submerged timber.

Even a tiny amount of salad dangling from the jig seems to discourage walleyes from striking. To avoid this, select a jig that has the eye positioned at the front of the lure. The most effective of these jigs are bullet shaped in order to cut thick weeds better than the bulky, round jig heads.

Casting Jigs

The various shapes and sizes of leadhead jigs can be fished in many different ways, but three primary methods characterize the most common ways to catch walleyes with jigs. Casting, dragging and swimming leadheads produce millions of fish for thousands of anglers annually.

Casting jigs tipped with minnows, nightcrawlers or leeches is one of the most exciting methods for fishing walleyes. Unfortunately, developing a highly refined "touch" for throwing jigs and working them back along the bottom requires a considerable amount of patience and practice.

The best jig casters are almost always those anglers who live in areas with abundant fish populations. Tournament professional Mike McClelland is a prime example. Hailed as one of the best jiggers in the nation, McClelland learned his trade fishing South Dakota's walleye-rich Lake Oahe. A Missouri-River-system reservoir, Lake Oahe harbors a tremendous amount of walleyes that are seemingly always willing to bite on a well-presented, jig-and-minnow combination.

McClelland started his tournament career as a bass angler. Mike's experience as a bass angler paved the way for his eventual success as a walleye fisherman who prefers to cast jigs for bottom-hugging fish.

"It was bass fishing that taught me how to control the boat with a bow-mounted electric motor," says McClelland. "Most of the popular bass-fishing presentations require the angler to position the boat a short distance from structure or cover and throw some type of lure into a group of feeding fish. It didn't take me long to realize this strategy is a deadly way to find and catch walleyes."

McClelland's early experiences with walleye fishing convinced him that casting jigs was one of the best ways to locate fish that other anglers were overlooking. "When I got into walleye fishing, most anglers fished jigs directly beneath the boat or dragged slip-sinker rigs around in fairly deep water," he explains. "Guides quickly locate these fish because deep-water walleyes are easy to spot and pin down with the help of a fishing graph."

Finding walleyes in reservoirs isn't difficult. Major points that taper into deep water seemingly attract every walleye in the vicinity. Guides and other anglers work over these points, concentrating on the fish they mark in water from 15 to 30 feet deep.

McClelland was one of the earliest walleye pioneers to discover that deep-water fish frequently move in shallow to feed. "I started discovering fish in water so shallow, the only way to reach them was with a silent electric motor and a long cast," he says. "I often fish the same points other anglers are working, but instead of working deep water, I fancast the top and edge of the points near shore."

Walleyes found in shallow water are aggressive and eager to bite. Finding and catching these shallow fish helped McClelland win many tournaments throughout the years.

McClelland's shallow-water jigging success has become legendary. For the most part, Mike's jigging success encompasses a three-part strategy: Lightweight jigs, thin fishing line and short fishing rods enable McClelland to refine a jig-casting system that's deadly wherever walleyes are found.

"Lightweight jigs are an important part of jigging success," he says. "Simply stated, light jigs are easier for a fish to inhale completely into its mouth than heavier jigs. Most of my jigging is done with ⅛- and ¼-ounce jigs."

Water depth, bait size and wind conditions all are factors considered by McClelland to determine the correct jig weight to use. In very shallow water when the wind isn't blowing, a 1/16-ounce jig may be the best possible choice. More difficult conditions, such as heavy winds, may force him to fish a ¼- or ⅜-ounce jig to maintain contact with the bottom.

The only way to effectively fish light jigs is with thin monofilament line. By using 4- or 6-pound-test monofilament, the angler can throw even 1/16-ounce jigs a considerable distance. Thin monofilament line also offers jigs greater freedom of movement or action.

"The rods used when throwing jigs are also critical," says McClelland. "Most anglers fish with 6- to 7-foot-long medium/light action rods. These sticks are fine for slip-sinker rigging or fishing bobbers, but they don't contain enough sensitivity to be good jig-pitching rods."

For throwing jigs, a spinning rod with a medium action that is approximately 5 to 5½ feet long is needed. Shorter and slightly stiffer rods help telegraph every movement of the jig along the bottom into the angler's hands.

"Anglers refer to 'feel' a lot when they talk about jigging for walleyes," says McClelland. "The truth is you can't feel a jig when it's falling through the water, you can't feel it resting on bottom and lots of times you don't even feel it when a walleye sucks the jig into its mouth. If you're lucky and your rod is sensitive, you'll feel a slight tick when the fish inhales the bait."

The rod's sensitivity and the angler's speed in setting the hook determines the number of strikes parlayed into numbers of fish hooked and landed. Using short, sensitive rods and setting the hook the instant he "feels" resistance have enabled McClelland to cash in on a bonanza of shallow-water walleyes.

Dragging Jigs

McClelland uses his electric motor to position his boat within casting distance of fish. Once he has located a school of walleyes, he uses his rod to cast and impart action to his jigs.

Some anglers, however, think casting wastes valuable fishing time. When the jig is in the air or being retrieved for another cast, it's not fishing. These anglers prefer to use a boat to pull or drag jigs along the bottom, keeping the bait within the strike zone.

An effective means of jigging for bottom-hugging walleyes, dragging jigs can be done by using an electric motor, small gasoline kicker engine, a main outboard or by simply drifting with the wind. Gary Roach, an award-winning tournament pro, has refined jig dragging into an effective walleye-fishing tactic. Like McClelland, Roach uses an electric motor to position his boat. Instead of fishing from the bow, however, Roach works off the back and uses a transom-mounted electric motor to pull the boat backward over bottom structure.

"I fish from the back of the boat for several reasons," says Roach. "Most importantly, I can control the boat best when I'm fishing off the back. Sitting near the transom, I'm in a comfortable position to make boat-control adjustments and study my electronics. Important fishing gear and bait are also at my fingertips."

Dragging jigs along the bottom requires a stand-up jig head. This Jig-A-Whopper Drip Lip jig sets in an upright position when at rest. The hook and bait are positioned off the bottom, making the bait easier for walleyes to spot and reducing the chances of snagging.

Roach looks for subtle changes in bottom structure which attract and concentrate walleyes. Slight depressions in the bottom, small rock piles, saddles between humps and other features catch Roach's eye. Often overlooked by others, these spots-on-the-spot are mini walleye-fishing gold mines for Roach.

"Dragging jigs or rigs over little mini-structure is my favorite and most productive angling technique," adds Roach. "I hunt for walleyes using my electronics, then use the boat to drag my jig through the fish. Periodically, I pump my jigs off bottom with short pops of the rodtip. This hopping-and-dragging motion seems to trigger a few more fish than simply letting the jig drag along bottom."

Swimming Jigs

Swimming a leadhead at mid-depth in the water column or through heavy cover is one of the least practiced forms of jigging. Often thought of as strictly bottom-fishing lures, modified versions of the common leadhead jig are equally effective on suspended walleyes or fish holding in thick cover, such as weeds or timber.

Lake Erie anglers proved decades ago that the weight-forward spinner is a highly effective tool for tempting suspended walleyes. Technically speaking, a weight-forward spinner is nothing more than a leadhead jig with a spinner blade to add flash and action.

Weight-forward spinners are fished by casting them and allowing the lure to sink for several seconds before beginning the retrieve. The longer the angler allows the lure to sink, the deeper the lure will run on the retrieve.

Anglers should count slowly as the lure is sinking. By experimenting and keeping track of the length of time the lure is allowed to sink, productive depth ranges can be determined. Once a productive depth or count is found, duplicating the same with additional casts is easy.

Various brands, sizes and models of weight-forward spinners are available. All accomplish the same basic task, yet many anglers have favorite models that seem to produce best. A modest selection of lures in ¼-, ⅜-, ½- and ⅝-ounce sizes is adequate to cover most weight-forward-spinner fishing situations.

Jig spinners, like weight-forwards, add a touch of fish-attracting flash to an otherwise boring jig presentation. Similar to the

The Weight-Forward Spinner

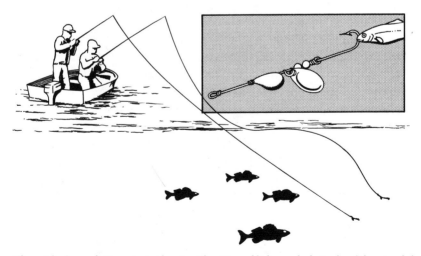

The weight-forward spinner is simply a jig with a spinner blade attached. Anglers fish suspended walleyes by casting the spinner forward, letting it sink and then slowly swimming it through the walleye school.

Some jigs are designed to move through the water in a swimming motion. This Northland Whistler Jig has a small blade that spins when the jig moves through the water. When walleyes are actively feeding, action-type jigs produce well.

spinnerbaits used by bass anglers, a jig spinner transforms a lead-head jig and a small safety-pin-style spinner into a snag-resistant lure that's ideal for fishing weeds and other cover.

Jig spinners are often used with live bait, a plastic grub body or both. When walleyes move into weeds or other heavy cover, these lures are often the only practical way to cover water quickly without the hassle of constant snagging.

A slow, steady retrieve produces plenty of walleyes; however, many anglers prefer to fish jig spinners by using an erratic stop-and-go action. Allowing the bait to stop and helicopter downward periodically can trigger explosive strikes from walleyes holding tight to cover.

Experimenting with different retrieves is the most productive way to fish jig spinners. Some days the fish slash at these lures, passing by at a steady and rapid pace. Other days the fish seem to prefer a bait that's slow-rolled near the bottom. The old standby stop-and-go, helicopter-style retrieve often works when everything else fails.

The ways and means of catching walleyes with jigs are numerous. For every style of leadhead jig there is a walleye-fishing presentation tailored toward tempting these tasty gamefish.

Casting and retrieving jigs along the bottom, dragging them in the sand or swimming them through open water are all effective ways to interest walleyes. Take your pick and go fishing. Thousands of walleye fanatics already have.

=12=

Slip-Sinker Rigging

Slip-sinker rigs and walleye fishing go together like the co-
medic duo of Abbott and Costello, except there's nothing funny about the way live-bait rigs perform on walleyes.
A serious fish-catching system, slip-sinker rigging has
earned the respect of virtually every angler across walleye wonderland. With the possible exception of leadhead jigs, no single walleye lure, presentation or angling method comes close to being
more popular or productive. Simple to learn, slip-sinker rigging
transforms basic angling skills into fish fillets.

Having the capability of feeding line to a fish after it bites is
the main difference between jigging and rigging. Rigging allows
the angler to detect the strike, then free-spool line to the fish
while it turns the bait in its mouth and swallows its prize.

While all this is happening, the fish doesn't feel any pressure
from the angler or weight of the sinker. After a few seconds, the
angler closes his reel bail, tightens up on the fish and smacks it
with a head-turning hookset.

To say rigging is a versatile walleye-fishing system would be a
serious understatement. Effective in shallow and deep water, in
weeds or rocks, on sand, gravel or clay bottoms, slip-sinker rigging
has few limits when walleyes are found near bottom structure.

Anyone can learn to catch walleyes using slip-sinker rigs. The
most skilled professionals and rank-amateurs alike find rigging a
productive way to fill a livewell.

The basic live-bait rigging system consists of a weight that

The king of rigging, Fishing Hall of Fame member Gary Roach (standing), taught Mark Martin and thousands of other anglers how to fish walleyes with slip-sinker rigs.

Slip-Sinker Rigging

Shown here are various slip-sinker rigging components. They include hooks, floating jig heads, snaps, weights and quick-change rigging clips.

slides along the line, a swivel or snap to stop the sinker, a short leader and a hook. Simple and effective, these live-bait rigs have never been more popular or effective.

Live-bait rigging is easy to learn, yet there are many facets of rigging that escape the attention of the average angler. Details including sinker types and sizes, leader lengths, floats, attractors, hooks and live-bait choices all influence the ultimate effectiveness of these rigs.

Weights For Rigging

Slip sinkers used for live-bait rigging haven't changed much since the Lindner brothers introduced the walking-style weight. Designed to slide over rocky bottoms with fewer annoying snags, the walking sinker continues to dominate the world of slip-weight rigging.

Elbow-shaped walking sinkers glide along scattered rock, sand, gravel or clay bottoms with ease. When the bottom becomes covered with weeds, walking sinkers start to fall into that not-so-hot category. Weeds quickly catch on these sinkers and foul an otherwise ideal presentation.

In weedy conditions, veteran riggers replace the walking-style sinker with a bullet weight like those used by plastic-worm fishermen. The sinker should be rigged so the pointed end slides cleanly through the weed stalks.

Rigging with a bullet weight works well in thin or scattered patches of weeds. Defined weed edges, such as those associated with hard- and soft-bottom transitions or breaklines, are another excellent application for bullet-weight rigging.

When you are faced with heavy weeds, however, it's best to switch to a completely different presentation. Pulling any kind of live-bait rig through dense patches of weeds will lead to more frustrations than fish.

In most rigging situations, the sinker's weight is more important than its shape. Depending upon the size of bait used, water depth, line diameter and trolling speed, one of six different sinker weights will produce best. The most successful riggers strive to perfect their presentations by using the minimum amount of weight needed to keep the bait on the bottom.

The most common sinker weights among walleye fishermen are models weighing from ⅛ to ¾ ounce. Unfortunately, there are no hard-and-fast guidelines for matching sinker weight to water depth. Too many variables exist which make it difficult to develop a dependable "no-brainer" system for riggers.

In general, most rig fishermen stick with a thin and flexible monofilament line such as 6- or 8-pound test. Heavier line would require more sinker weight in order to maintain contact with the bottom. Lighter line—less than 6-pound test—leads to frequent break-offs and other line-abrasion problems.

More than half the rigging situations encountered in rivers, natural lakes and reservoirs require ¼- or ⅜-ounce rigging weights. Occasionally, heavier weights are needed to fish deeper water or maintain bottom contact during faster trolling.

With these guidelines in mind, anglers should stock up heavily on the ¼-, ⅜- and ½-ounce sizes, and have a modest assortment of lighter and heavier sinkers for special situations. Walking-style sinkers also come in bright colors and nifty plastic coatings. Remember, plastic-coated slip sinkers have more bulk so you have to go a little heavier in weight to accomplish the same objective as with uncoated models.

Painted sinkers may or may not make any difference. Cer-

The Bullet Weight

A bullet weight is a good substitute for the walking-style sinker when rigging in weeds. The pointed bullet weight pulls through weeds with fewer hang-ups.

tainly the addition of color can't hurt, but it does add a few more pennies to the cost of rig components. The new quick-change-style rigging systems are more practical and interesting than painted rigging weights.

A number of manufacturers offer rigging systems that allow the angler to replace the sinker with a lighter or heavier model without having to cut and retie the rig. Some weights feature an eye that is easily bent open and closed as needed to change the weight. Others incorporate a special rigging clip that accepts different sinkers designed to snap in and out of the clip. Either way, the idea of making it easy to change weights has great merit.

Leader Lengths
The length of leader used for slip-sinker rigging can be the difference between success and failure. As with sinker weights, there are no absolutes regarding leader lengths, and the topic is frequently debated.

In general, short leads seem to work well in murky water. The clearer the water becomes, however, the longer a leader must be to produce consistent results.

Obviously, there are limits to leader length. Approximately 18 inches is probably the shortest practical leader length for use with slip-sinker rigs. At the other extreme, 84 inches (7 feet) is about the maximum length that's practical to use with normal spinning tackle. The most commonly used lead lengths are probably 24, 36, 48 and 60 inches.

Leader length determines, in part, how far the bait rides off the bottom. Many anglers believe that using longer leaders will help suspend their baits in front of fish holding off the bottom. However, simply fishing a long leader does not guarantee that the bait will be suspended. Other factors, including the type of bait, trolling speed and the possible use of floats, influence the amount of bait lift.

The forward motion of the boat (trolling) has the strongest influence on how far off the bottom the bait rides. A brisk trolling speed creates water resistance that pins the bait tight to the bottom, regardless of lead length. In comparison, slow trolling speeds coupled with long leaders allow a limited amount of bait lift.

Therefore, anglers who are determined to fish their bait slightly off the bottom are forced to troll slowly with long leaders. In order to further increase bait lift, you can add small floats to the line.

Summing up the leader length discussion is not easy. Traditionalists prefer relatively short leaders because "short leads offer the best bait control and feel." The latest generation of live-bait riggers are going to longer leaders, arguing that extended leads produce better on finicky or heavily fished walleyes.

Adding Floats, Spinners, Attractors

Floating jig heads, in-line snell floats, float-and-spins, spinner blades, colorful beads and an endless variety of other attractors commonly find their way onto a slip-sinker rig. Depending upon their function, these additions to the leader are classified as either a floater or attractor, but, ironically, some of these are both.

Floating jig heads and floating spinners are two perfect examples. Designed to give the bait more lift off the bottom, floating jigs and floating spinners also provide some added action, color and flash.

The variety of floaters available is mind-boggling. Plain floating jig heads, floating jigs that wobble, soft-bodied floating jigs,

Bait Location When Rigging

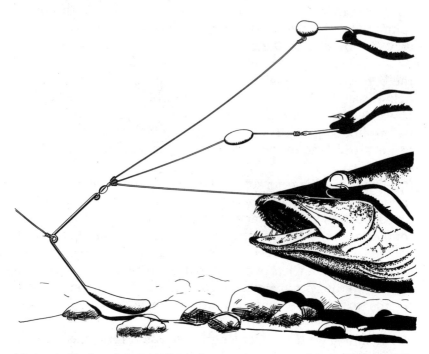

The length of leader and the type of hook, floats or other attractors determine how far off the bottom the bait will ride during rigging. It always depends upon the angler's presentation.

in-line snell floats and dozens of other devices that add buoyancy are waiting on tackle-shop peg hooks for anglers to try.

Size has a lot to do with how much lift floaters provide. Some floats, such as the in-line version, are small and provide only a limited amount of lift to small baits, such as tiny minnows or leeches. Others, such as the oversized wobbling jig head, can float large minnows, such as chubs or suckers, farther off the bottom.

In addition to positioning the bait somewhere off the bottom, floats can also add fish-catching slack to the leader. To fully appreciate how floats help the rig fisherman, you have to understand how walleyes feed.

Walleyes inhale their prey in much the same way as do bass. Like a vacuum cleaner picking up spilled popcorn, walleyes suck up morsels of food by flaring their gills and inhaling water into their mouths. The gills act somewhat like prison bars, preventing small baitfish and other tasty tidbits from escaping out through the gill cover.

Walleyes attempting to eat minnows attached to slip-sinker rigs often find it difficult to inhale such a seemingly easy target. Imagine a walleye trying to inhale the bait as the live-bait rig is slowly pulled away from the fish. If the bait is moving, the leader is taunt. Unless the fish can suck hard enough to pull the sinker off the bottom, it probably won't be able to inhale what seems like an easy meal.

Unless the leader has a little slack, walleyes may have trouble inhaling the bait. In-line floats help add a small degree of slack.

A small float midway along the snell causes the leader to bend slightly in the middle, creating slack in the leader. When a walleye inhales the bait, the bait and hook will flow freely into the fish's mouth because of the slack.

Pumping the rod is another way to add slack periodically to the leader. Pulling the rodtip slightly toward you, then dropping the rod back creates a pause in the forward motion of the rig. A slight pause gives interested walleyes opportunity to overtake and inhale the bait without feeling the weight's resistance.

In other words, taking steps that make it easy for fish to eat the bait is one of the most important aspects of live-bait rigging.

Various attractors can have a strong triggering effect on walleyes. Attractors fall into the same category of abundance as floats. From a simple colored bead to flashy spinner blades, anglers can choose from dozens of attractors designed to catch a walleye's attention.

A colorful glass or plastic bead threaded on the line emphasizes what live-bait rigging is all about. Simple, yet effective, a tiny bead adds an attracting color to an otherwise perfectly natural bait.

Flamboyant attractors, such as spinner blades, floating spins and rattle spins, are another important aspect of live-bait rigging. Spinners are powerful fish attractors.

Available in many sizes, shapes and color patterns, blade-style spinners are the most popular. Colorado- and Indiana-style blades are used the most by walleye fishermen; however, willow-leaf, French-style and even the June-Bug-style spinners take their share of fish.

In-Line Float

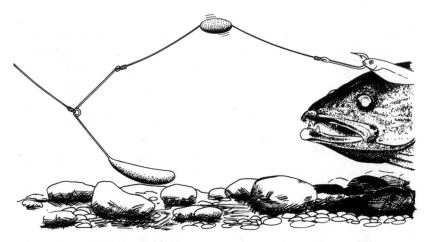

Adding an in-line float puts a small amount of slack in the line. This helps ensure that a walleye can inhale the bait completely into its mouth.

With the exception of in-line spinners, most spinner blades are connected to the line by means of a clevis which rotates around the line or leader. Different styles of clevises are available, including quick-change versions in which the blades can be changed without cutting the leader. Quick-change-style clevises are very popular when combined with walleye spinners. Being able to instantly change blade size, style or color is a real advantage.

When you're fishing metal spinner blades, place one or more snell floats between the blade and hook. Spinner blades must be trolled at a steady pace to keep the blade thumping properly; if the forward motion of the boat hesitates, the spinner stops turning and sinks to the bottom. Even a slight hesitation, such as making a turn, can cause the blades to sink and the hooks to snag bottom. Keeping the bait from dragging on the bottom also prevents debris from fouling the bait or clogging the clevis.

Hooks And Bait

Naturally, the size of bait used when rigging influences the choice of hooks. Small baits such as leeches or 'crawlers require compact hooks. A No. 4 Beak- or Viking-style hook is an excellent choice. Small enough to be hidden in a leech or 'crawler, these hooks also have a wide gap between hook point and shank. This results in a higher ratio of hooked and landed fish.

Larger baits such as suckers, chubs and other chunky minnows require bigger hooks. A No. 2 Beak hook works well on minnows; however, many anglers prefer using even larger No. 1 or 1/0 Aberdeen hooks. These hooks have a wider hook gap and are made from thin wire that will readily penetrate a walleye's bony mouth.

Another advantage of the Aberdeen hooks is that they are easily bent if you snag the bottom. Simply apply enough pressure to bend open the hook and retrieve the rig. The bent hook can be reshaped with a pair of pliers, touched up with a file, rebaited and put back to use. After all, the time saved tying on new rigs is additional fishing time.

Aberdeen hooks probably would be the all-around best for rigging if nightcrawlers weren't so long. Putting a single Aberdeen hook through the nose of a 'crawler is just begging for short bites and half-eaten 'crawlers.

Because 'crawlers are such a long bait, many anglers use two Beak- or Viking-style hooks snell-knotted 3 to 6 inches apart to fish them. A two-hook rig acts like a stinger hook, catching the short-biters.

Regardless of the hook style used, all rigging hooks must be sticky sharp. The very nature of live-bait rigging results in more line being let out than for other fishing methods. The amount of stretch in thin monofilament line makes it difficult to pound a dull hook home. Even hooks taken directly from the package could benefit from a little "touch up" with a small file. Fish hooks can never be too sharp.

One of the most popular walleye-fishing methods since the introduction of split shot and hook, slip-sinker rigging has a rich history and thriving future in walleye fishing.

=13=

Bottom Bouncers

ottom-bouncer sinkers are at once unique, versatile and effective. The wire and lead contraptions collectively known as bottom bouncers may be the most important terminal-tackle advancement to hit the walleye scene since the fish hook. Even though bottom-bouncer sinkers vary somewhat in shape, size and design, the function of this weight system remains the same. A chunk of lead molded midway along a piece of wire keeps the bait on the bottom.

The wire helps the weight ride along the bottom and flow smoothly over snags. This system has an advantage in that it follows changes in depth contours and imparts a seductive stop-and-go action to the bait that other sinkers can't match.

Born along the banks of the Missouri River, bottom-bouncer sinkers are standard equipment on walleye boats in the plains states of North Dakota, South Dakota, Wyoming, Nebraska and Kansas. However, anglers in Michigan, Wisconsin, Minnesota, Ohio, Pennsylvania and Indiana have only recently discovered the many ways bottom bouncers can help put more walleyes in their boats. In Canadian Shield lakes and in most other areas, bottom bouncers are a rare sight.

Proof that necessity is the mother of invention, the bottom bouncers evolved because anglers needed a snagless weight that would stay on the bottom even while being pulled over various bottom types and contours. The reservoir systems on the Missouri River became the proving grounds for a fishing system that has

There's nothing basic about bottom bouncers. These unique bottom-fishing weights have taken the world of walleye fishing by storm. Versatile and effective, bottom bouncing is becoming the preferred method of fishing structure walleyes in North America.

Bottom Bouncers

How Bottom Bouncers Work

Bottom bouncers slide over rocks and other bottom debris with ease. As the sinker passes over the debris, a rocking motion causes the bait to hesitate and flutter downward, then speed forward again. When fishing bottom bouncers, the bait fluctuates from right on the bottom to a foot or so above it.

since proved to be effective wherever walleyes are found holding near the bottom.

Reservoir anglers needed a weight system that could pull night-crawler harnesses and other live-bait rigs over rock-covered flats and along deep-water points and sunken islands.

Bottom Bouncers And Spinners

When a walleye angler says he's catching fish on spinners, he's probably not talking about the famous French-bladed variety. Walleye anglers collectively refer to the many forms of the common nightcrawler harness as spinner rigs. The variations of available spinner rigs are too numerous to list, but a typical spinner consists of a 36- to 60-inch monofilament leader armed with two baitholder-style hooks snelled on one end, a few colorful plastic beads added in front of the hook and a Colorado- or Indiana-style spinner blade that rotates on a small metal clevis.

When baited with a fat 'crawler and attached to a bottom-bouncer weight being drifted or trolled along the bottom, this common walleye presentation becomes a deadly fishing tool. Hundreds of walleye-fishing guides and thousands of their customers would cheerfully agree. This presentation produces!

Three noteworthy changes in spinner design have evolved in recent years. Tournament professional Gary Parsons learned to fish spinners in the Dakotas during the days when it took more than 80 pounds of fish to win the annual Governor's Cup tournament.

"During the early years of tournament fishing, spinner rigs were tied using abrasion resistant 20- to 30-pound-test monofilament," explains Parsons. "Crude by modern standards, these snelled spinners were built to last but not to provide that critical fluttering action. Spinners tied on stiff monofilament seriously reduce the amount of fish-catching action when the rig is pulled along in a stop-and-go motion."

Parsons began experimenting with hand-tied spinners made

Bottom bouncers and spinners go together like pie and ice cream. An assortment of different sized and colored spinner blades, clevises and hooks is all the angler needs to tie up his own customized spinner rigs.

with 10-pound-test monofilament. It didn't take long for him to realize his homemade spinners were outfishing the traditional tackle-store variety. Today, most walleye pros select spinner rigs that are tied using 10- to 14-pound-test fishing line.

Clevises—the little devices that hold the spinner blades on the line—became the next important advancement to hit the spinner fishing scene. A plastic clevis with which an angler could quickly change blades knocked the walleye-fishing world on its oar a few years ago. For the first time, an angler could change blade size, shape or color without having to change the entire spinner rig. So popular is this little piece of plastic that other lure companies have begun using modified versions of the clevis on live-bait rigs, spinnerbaits, weight-forward spinners and in-line spinners.

Hook spacing is a subtle yet important improvement in spinner rigs. Most commercially produced spinners come with two hooks spaced approximately 3 inches apart. When these spinners are baited with a healthy nightcrawler, more than half of the bait stretches behind the last hook. Short strikes and missed fish are the result. Increasing the hook spacing from 3 to 6 inches has the same effect as adding a stinger hook.

Tying Your Own Spinners

Collectively, these improvements have led tackle manufacturers to build and sell spinner rigs that are far superior to those available just a few years ago. Still, many anglers prefer to tie their own spinners. Spinner components, such as blades, clevises, hooks and beads, are available at most tackle shops.

Making your own spinners is easy and fun. A few winter evenings spent tying spinners provides the angler with an ample supply of these fish-catching, live-bait rigs come walleye season. No special tools are needed, but the angler must master one knot to build the best spinners.

The common snell knot is used in tying most live-bait rigs. Snell knots are easy to tie, strong and help position hooks at precise intervals.

When snelling a spinner, start with a pre-cut length of 10- to 14-pound-test monofilament. Most anglers prefer a finished spinner of 36 to 60 inches. Allow a few extra inches of monofilament to make up for the length of line used in tying knots.

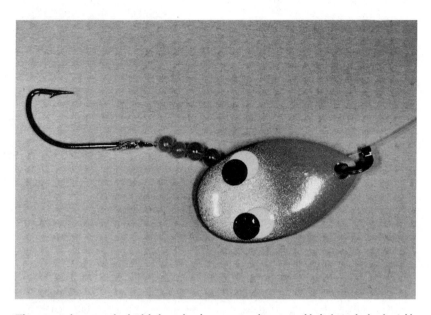

This spinner has several colorful plastic beads separating the spinner blade from the hook. Adding beads prevents the spinner from hitting the leech, minnow or 'crawler when being pulled through the water.

Abrasion-resistant or extra-tough fishing lines are preferred over limp lines. Soft lines are easily damaged when the metal clevis and spinner blade rotate around the line. So use the snell knot described in Chapter 9 to attach a live-bait or baitholder-style hook that has a turned up eye.

To add a second or third hook, simply thread another hook onto the line, space the hooks accordingly, and begin wrapping the monofilament around the shank as before.

When the hooks are tied in place, various colorful beads, floats, blades and other attractions can be threaded onto the line. Finish the rig by tying a simple, double, overhand loop knot in the end or tie on a barrel swivel.

Other Effective Bottom-Bouncer Rigs

Spinners are one of the most common live-bait rigs used with bottom bouncers; however, well-rounded anglers depend upon several other rigging options. The simplest of all bottom-bouncer rigs consists of a 36- to 60-inch-monofilament leader armed with a No. 2 Aberdeen-style hook. This bottom-bouncing rig is ideally suited for working minnows, 'crawlers or leeches among pockets of walleyes found holding on prominent structure. Sunken islands, point-tips stretching out into deep water and the bases of fast-sloping breaks are prime examples. Canadian Shield lakes and many reservoirs frequently offer this type of opportunity.

This simple hook-and-leader, live-bait rig works best in situations where the fish are holding tight to a specific spot or spot-on-the-spot. When walleyes hold tight to structure, an accurate and slow presentation is often required to trigger strikes.

An electric or small gasoline kicker motor is used to slowly drag this bottom-bouncer rig along prominent fish-holding sites. At such slow speeds, spinners or other action-type attractors wouldn't have the proper action. A small float threaded midway onto the leader makes it easier for walleyes to fully inhale the bait.

Bottom Bouncers And Boards

Most bottom-bouncer rigs can be used with in-line planer boards. Using boards to spread out a trolling pattern for covering large flats or reefs makes sense. Combining bottom bouncers with boards is the least practiced of all bottom-rigging methods. Ironically, linking bottom bouncers and in-line skis may be the most effective rigging option of all!

Bottom bouncers with spinner rigs, shallow-diving crankbaits, flutter spoons and simple hook-and-live-bait leaders are all more effective when combined with in-line planers. Using side planers to spread the trolling lines increases the odds of contacting fish and makes wiring up an effective pattern easier.

Many different in-line boards are available. Individual boards may have different release systems, but the function of all side planers remains the same.

To rig bottom bouncers with in-line boards, let out enough line to keep the sinker dragging along the bottom at the desired trolling speed. Then attach the line to the side planer release and tighten the release so the board cannot easily release the line. When attached properly, the board will remain on the line until the angler removes it to check the bait or fight the fish.

Once the board is securely attached to the line, drop it in the water and allow the board to plane out to the side. Let out enough line so the board runs from 25 to 75 feet to the side of the boat. When the first line is set, place the rod in a holder and begin putting out additional lines.

Bottom bouncers add a stop-and-go action to live-bait rigs that triggers fish when other angling presentations fail. The cam action of the wire bottom-bouncer arm rocking back and forth over bottom debris causes the bait to hesitate momentarily.

Bottom Bouncers

Bottom Bouncing With Boards

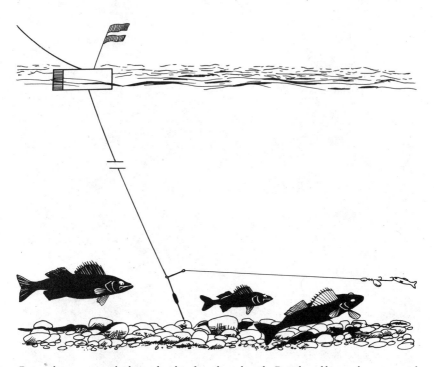

Bottom bouncers can also be used with in-line planer boards. Boards and bottom bouncers work best on flats that have few snags.

Once all lines are set and running properly, you must watch the boards carefully. As the bottom bouncers slide over the bottom, they'll hang up momentarily before pulling free and continuing. When this happens, the boards dart backward sharply, then continue running normally.

When a fish is hooked, the board will respond by sliding backward in a smooth and steady motion. The boards actually help the angler see the strike!

When a walleye is hooked, the board must first be reeled in and removed. Once the release on the side planer is removed from the line, the fight continues until the fish is landed.

Using this in-line board method, two or more lines can be easily fished per side. When a fish is hooked on an outside line, the inside board must be reeled in first to prevent tangled lines.

There's no need to remove the board from the inside line. Simply reel it in and lay the rod down along the opposite side of the boat until the fish on the outside board is landed. With the walleye safely in the boat, reset the board that was cleared. This board becomes the outside line, and the line that caught the fish is reset on the inside.

Leapfrogging lines helps keep the maximum amount of rigs in the water at all times. It's a wise idea to check all lines frequently. Perch and other panfish have a nasty habit of nipping at the bait or getting hooked themselves. The only way to know if the bait has been stolen or taken by a small panfish is to check the lines every few minutes.

Versatile, effective and simple to fish, bottom bouncers have a bright future in walleye fishing. Combined with live-bait rigs or artificial hardware, these odd-looking combinations of wire and lead appear to be worthless. In reality, they may well be the best buy a walleye fisherman can make.

=====14=====

Slip-Bobbering Tricks

Often considered children's toys, slip bobbers are a serious fishing tool. In fact, slip bobbers are the ultimate depth-control aid. Corks, floats or bobbers—whatever you call these ingenious fishing aids—provide walleye anglers with a new dimension to live-bait rigging. Suspending fresh bait in front of a walleye's nose may be the most deadly presentation possible. Bobbers are fun to rig and fish. They make it easy to see when you've got a bite.

Float-fishing's greatest advantage is that anyone can learn to rig and fish slip bobbers effectively. Bobbers add the dimension of sight to walleye fishing. Few other angling presentations allow the angler to actually "see" the fish bite. Slip bobbers also are the perfect fishing method for children and other rookies who have little confidence in jigging, rigging and other traditional walleye-fishing methods. Watching a bobber wobble and then go under is a thrill to any angler.

Sight-fishing is an important element of slip-bobbering. The extended length of presentation that bobber-fishing offers also is significant. A slip bobber puts live bait in front of a walleye's nose and keeps it there for quite some time. Even the most negative-minded walleye has a difficult time turning down a squirming leech, panicking minnow or undulating 'crawler.

Basic Rigging Methods
Rigging a slip bobber is simple and easy. The basic compo-

Often thought of as toys or panfish rigs, slip bobbers are serious walleye-fishing aids. A slip bobber enables an angler to fish areas that would be impossible to fish with conventional tackle. Shallow or deep, slip bobbers are deadly walleye producers.

Slip-Bobbering Tricks   143

nents include a float, bobber stop, split shot and hook. The bobber stop is the first component to be placed on the line.

Even though many different types of bobber stops exist, they all provide the same basic function. The bobber stop slides along the line, enabling the angler to preset any fishing depth desired. A good bobber stop should slide on the line with a little fingertip pressure; it should stay in place once the correct depth has been reached.

The most popular bobber stop is made from Dacron line, tied around a small tube. The fishing line then is run through the bobber stop tube and the Dacron-line knot is slid off onto the line. The plastic tube is discarded and Dacron material's tag ends are cinched up to tighten the small knot on the line. Finally, the tag ends are clipped, making a clean knot that will stop the bobber and yet flow easily through the rod guides. Some anglers add a small plastic bead as insurance that the bobber stop won't pass through the bobber.

Now the slip bobber is added to the line. Many different shapes and sizes of wood, plastic or foam slip bobbers are available, giving the angler plenty of options.

The float's material is less important than its shape. Wide-bodied floats are very buoyant, making it difficult for walleyes to pull them under. Thinner, cigar-shaped floats are preferred because they cast like a bullet and will dip underwater at the slightest tug.

Most slip floats must be threaded onto the line; however, a few models can be clipped or snapped over the line and are convenient when the bobber-fishing rod is also used for other presentations. Weight must be added to the line to sink the bait and make the bobber stand upright in the water. Several small split shots are normally pinched on the line, approximately 12 inches above the bait. It's important to use enough split shot so the bobber rides low in the water with only the top of the float visible. Balancing the float causes it to sink at the slightest pressure. Light-biting walleyes often drop the bait if they feel any type of resistance.

Some bobbers have a small lead ring mounted on the bottom of the float. This weight is designed to help counterbalance the float and make casting easier. Even weighted bobbers usually need an extra shot to balance them perfectly.

Balancing Your Float

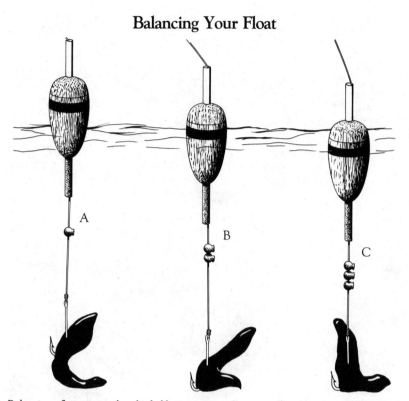

Balancing a float is critical to slip-bobbering success. For example, with only one shot (A), this float is too buoyant. Attaching two shots (B) is better; however, the float is still too buoyant. Adding a third shot (C) is best because only the top of the float is visible; now it will sink with the slightest nibble.

The types of hooks used for slip-bobber fishing is almost limitless. One of the most unusual hooks is the new wide bend. Wide-bend hooks are designed particularly for vertical presentations. The open sprout of these hooks offers exceptionally good hooking ratios during vertical hooksets. Because of the shape of these hooks, anglers are able to use a smaller hook size.

Many anglers prefer using small leadhead jigs instead of single hooks. A jig keeps the bait horizontal in the water and doubles as a counterbalancing weight.

Anglers who fish bobbers in thick weed tangles are especially partial to jig heads. A jig's weight takes the bait down into the weed cover and prevents an active minnow or leech from winding the line around weed stems.

At other times, however, it's important to have the bait mov-

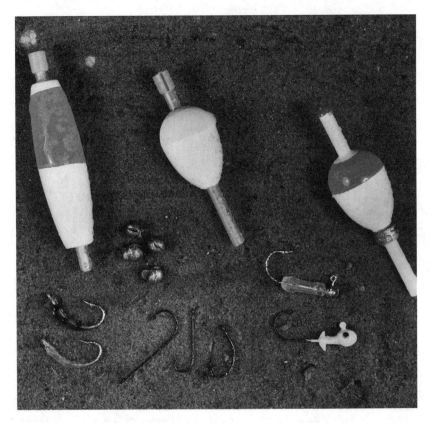

A small selection of slip bobbers and terminal rigging gear should be in every walleye-fishing tackle box. A weighted bobber (right) is easier to cast in strong winds.

ing around freely. Anglers using single hooks often adjust the position of their split shots, giving the bait more or less freedom of movement.

A split shot pinched on the line 3 inches above a squirming leech doesn't give the leech enough slack to attract walleyes. Sliding the shot 12 inches or more up the line provides active baits, like minnows and leeches, more room in which to do their job.

Fishing The Weeds

Weedy lakes are prime bobber-fishing targets. In most lakes, walleyes will use weed cover more than reefs, points or other classic bottom structure. Weeds provide an ideal habitat for walleyes. Ambush feeders by nature, walleyes lie in wait along weedlines or in dense stands of aquatic cover. When minnows or other tasty tidbits pass by, walleyes simply rush out and grab a quick meal.

Lakes with dense cabbage stands or other broad-leaf, submergent weed cover are difficult to fish with jigs, rigs or crankbaits.

A slip bobber is the ultimate vertical presentation for working weedlines or patches of thick aquatic vegetation. An electric motor and a pair of polarized fishing glasses are valuable aids for slip-bobbering the weeds.

An electric motor is ideal for quietly moving the boat while you're hunting for productive-looking weed edges or pockets. Polarized glasses make it easier to see submerged weedtops below the surface of the water.

When searching for weeds, get as high above the water's surface as you can. Stand on the casting deck, boat seat, cooler or anything that will give you a better vantage point. Once productive-looking weeds are located, work the electric motor to properly position the boat.

You want your boat within an easy lob cast of the weeds. Lob casting the bobber rig is less likely to cause the minnow to be torn free during the cast, and the softer bobber landing is less likely to spook feeding fish.

Choose an opening in the weeds and flip the bobber rig onto it. Start with the bait within 12 inches of the bottom; later, you may want to try suspending the bait farther off the bottom.

Resist the temptation to sit tight and wait for something to happen. The secret to fishing the weeds with slip bobbers is to keep moving until a group of fish is located. Cruise along silently with the electric motor and toss bobber rigs into other likely spots. If no bites occur within a couple of minutes, reel in, check the bait and make another cast. It's necessary to fish with fresh and lively bait at all times. A dead minnow or limp leech won't interest many walleyes.

Minnows usually are the best live bait for fishing weeds. Other species, including perch, bluegills and bullheads, also inhabit the weeds. Panfish will usually ignore a good-sized minnow, but a 'crawler or leech will attract every pesky panfish in the vicinity.

Reefs, Points And Sunken Structure

Classic walleye bottom structure, including reefs, sunken islands and dominant lake points, are ideal places, too, for using slip bobbers. Many times these types of structure will show up in shallow water. Even though walleyes aren't shy about using these shallow food shelves, approaching them with traditional angling methods can be difficult.

Pulling rigs or dragging jigs over this type of shallow structure is sure to spook more walleyes than you will catch. Anchoring upwind of the structure and drifting slip bobbers into position is often the best possible way to catch these fish.

To fish bobbers effectively on isolated bottom structure, you must anchor your boat correctly. The problem is that most anglers are not prepared to anchor a boat securely.

Too small an anchor and too little anchor rope are the most common reasons for poor anchoring. The typical walleye-fishing boat requires a 25- to 28-pound, navy-type anchor to hold it in a stiff breeze. Navy anchors work best on all bottom types; however, some of the new collapsible fluke-style anchors are also worth a try. Use plenty of ½- to ⅝-inch, smooth nylon rope for anchoring—a minimum amount of rope for secure anchoring is 100 feet and 150 feet would be even better. A long rope helps the anchor bite and hold in a strong wind, and it allows more flexibility in boat positioning.

Before anchoring the boat, drop a small marker buoy over the structure you want to fish. Move upwind of the structure and carefully lower the anchor off the bow. Let out enough rope so the anchor can bite into the bottom solidly. Once the anchor grabs hold, continue to let out rope until the boat is within casting distance of the marker buoy.

Now let the wind drift the bobbers into position. As the boat sways back and forth on the anchor rope, you can fish a large area in a short period of time. The harder the wind blows, the better this shallow-water structure-fishing becomes. This is because wave action disorients baitfish and provides walleyes with a feeding bonanza.

Minnows are a good choice for this type of fishing. Hook the minnow lightly through both lips. A hardy minnow, such as a fathead or spottail shiner, is more likely to survive repeated casts and provide maximum action.

Leeches are also excellent live bait, especially during the summer months when minnows are difficult to keep alive. Leeches should be hooked through the sucker or wide end. Hooked in this manner the leech swims invitingly away from the hook.

When walleyes are found shallow, casting slip-bobber rigs is an excellent way to reach spooky walleyes. Keith Kavajecz took this healthy walleye in 3 feet of water using a slip float and a 7-foot, rod-and-reel combination.

Slip-Bobbering Tricks

Bobbers And The Wind

When fishing with bobbers, use the wind to your advantage. Anchor upwind of bottom struc-
ture and let the wind drift the bobber rig into the shallow structure.

Nightcrawlers are also excellent summer slip-bobber bait. The 'crawler can be hooked through the nose or in the middle. Hooking the 'crawler in the middle produces a desirable double-tail effect that really attracts walleyes.

Slip Bobbers In Rivers
One of the most overlooked walleye-fishing tools, slip bobbers are deadly river-fishing aids. In a drifting or anchored position, bobbers offer the necessary depth control while reducing the chances of your bait snagging bottom.

Shallow flats, holes, sunken timber and steep banks that drop off sharply into deep water are just a few of the river-fishing situations suited for slip-bobber fishing.

When drift fishing, cast the bobber perpendicular to the boat and current or slightly downstream. Casting upstream of a drifting boat results in the boat dragging the bobber downstream and lifting the bait off the bottom.

When fishing from an anchored boat, always cast the bobber upstream and let the current wash the float toward the boat. Keep the line taunt but not tight against the bobber as it drifts downstream. If the line has some slack, the bobber may not show subtle strikes as well, and it's difficult to set the hook with authority.

Many bobber fishermen use long rods to reduce line slack. A rod used for steelhead fishing is also an excellent slip-bobber rod for walleyes. Rods that are 8 to 10 feet long control the slack better during the hookset and keep more line out of the water.

Whether their boats are drifting or anchored, veteran bobber fishermen watch their floats intently. The float's attitude keeps the angler informed of the location of his bait in relation to the bottom.

If the bobber tilts or bobs back and forth frequently, the weight is probably dragging along the bottom. If the bobber never moves, the weight may be too far off bottom to tempt strikes. Trial-and-error is the only effective way to master depth control when fishing bobbers.

A leadhead jig is the ideal terminal hook for river slip-bobber fishing. Jigs position the bait in a natural, horizontal position and make it easy to keep the bait tight to the bottom. The ideal slip-bobber rig for rivers presents the bait within 3 to 6 inches of the bottom. Few fish will be taken if the bait is farther up.

15

Effectively Fishing Rivers

Moving water presents an angling opportunity that few walleye anglers utilize. North America has no shortage of excellent walleye flowages, yet the vast majority of those who chase walleyes avoid rivers like a stray hound avoids the dog catcher. River walleye anglers can usually be divided into two distinctively different groups. The first, perhaps best known as river rats, fish rivers with a passion and confidence that only comes from many hours of experience on flowing water. The second consists of anglers who primarily chase walleyes in natural inland lakes and rarely deal with strong currents, so they are often out of their element when faced with a raging river.

The strengths and weaknesses of each of these two groups of anglers are apparent on the walleye tournament circuit. With few exceptions, anglers who fare well in river-based tournaments struggle in contests held on natural lakes or reservoirs. On the other hand, lake-fishing purists often fail miserably in river-based tournaments.

The reasons lake-fishing specialists struggle on rivers are as numerous as the lakes they prefer to fish. Simply stated, many of the traditional rules of walleye fishing simply don't apply to rivers. Moving water makes for more difficult boat control, accurate lure presentation and fish-finding.

It's true, rivers do present some unique challenges. Controlling a fishing boat in current requires specialized equipment that

Beautiful scenery surrounds a typical Midwestern walleye river. To say that rivers are fertile walleye factories is a serious understatement. Some of the best walleye fishing in North America centers around flowing water.

Effectively Fishing Rivers

many anglers don't own or can't afford. Learning to deal with the current instead of fighting it also takes some patience and time to master.

To top it off, river walleyes and sauger are less likely to be found in the same spot two days in a row than their lake-loving cousins. Walleyes that take up residence along typical lake structure or cover tend to be homebodies. Seasonal changes force these fish to move in search of food; yet it's not uncommon for a school of walleyes to use the same structure or weed cover for several weeks.

Pinpointing river walleyes isn't always so easy. Moving current and rising or falling water levels are constantly influencing the location of baitfish. Ultimately, these unpredictable forces cause walleyes and other predatory fish to follow the wandering schools of forage. Exactly where a school of river walleyes will turn up is anyone's guess.

The "where" factor in walleye fishing is always important, but it's never more critical to success than with rivers. Though finding river walleyes may require extra effort, finding a productive fishing hole is likely to result in a yield of numerous fish within a short period of time.

Finding River Walleyes

Pinpointing and ultimately catching river walleyes boils down to a simple two-part strategy. Recognizing the many slack-water areas in the current that attract baitfish is important in locating walleyes. Seldom will walleyes be found far from a readily available food source. Once these slack-water areas are identified, finding fish in them is simply a matter of checking as many likely spots as possible until fish are found.

Commonly referred to as current breaks, the slack-water areas of a river take on many forms. Anything jutting out into the flow of water, such as a point, fallen tree or wing dam, may represent a fishing hotspot. Water swirls around these obstructions and forms a slack-water area or eddy directly downstream. Also, a small slack-water area is formed along the front faces of wing dams, attracting walleyes during normal and low-water levels.

Obstructions on the bottom, such as rock piles, submerged stumps or logs, also form current breaks. Most submerged features can be located by watching for bubbles on the water's surface.

Wing-Dam Walleyes

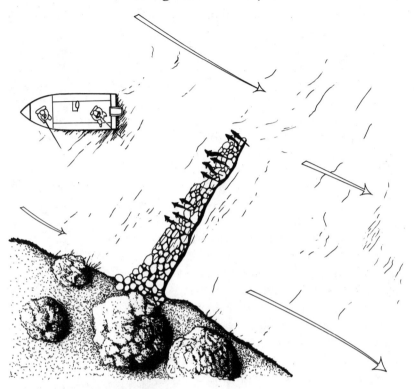

Irregularities along wing dams often hold the best concentrations of fish. Walleyes can be found concentrated on the front face of a wing dam by rocks which contact the bottom.

Still other current breaks that attract walleyes are natural depressions along the bottom and outside river bends that, through time, have been scoured out with deep holes.

Finally, wide stretches of river flats where there is slower current can also attract large numbers of walleyes. These flats can be especially good producers in the spring if they're dotted with patches of gravel, rock or rubble suitable for spawning.

Many angling methods can be utilized to catch walleyes holding in these slack-water areas. Vertical jigging and working the front face of wing dams are two of the most efficient and popular river-fishing strategies.

Vertical Jigging

Almost anyone who has fished a river has probably worked a

jig directly beneath the boat. This simple jigging style enables the angler to feel the lure while keeping the bait in constant contact with the bottom.

Jigging beneath the boat is perhaps the most common river-fishing technique, yet few anglers ever graduate to the "major leagues" of vertical jigging. A refined form of vertical jigging dubbed "chasing the line" is one of the most deadly forms of river jigging. This specialized jigging method combines light line, light jigs and precise boat control into a jigging system that must be seen in action to be fully appreciated.

The angler uses an electric motor to continuously position the boat over the top of the jig. Without this boat-control aid, keeping the jig directly beneath the boat is nearly impossible in deep water or swift current.

The culprit on the river is wind—not current speed. Even a slight breeze causes the boat to drift faster or slower than the current. When this occurs, the jig's downstream drift becomes radically different from that of the boat, and the line starts to angle away from the all-important vertical position.

When the angler's line begins to show a sharp angle, the vertical presentation is lost and, in many cases, so is contact with the bottom. In order to keep the jig directly beneath the boat, the angler is forced to reposition the boat.

To the casual observer, moving the jig under the boat may seem easy. Unfortunately, physically moving the jig under the boat is all but impossible. However, positioning the boat over the top of the jig is easy—with the help of an electric motor.

To keep the jigs perfectly vertical as the boat drifts downstream, the angler must constantly move the boat over the top of the jig or "chase the line" to make allowances for wind drift. In essence, the angler is working to keep the boat drifting along at exactly the same speed as the current. Although the process sounds complicated, a little practice and a few pointers will have most anglers enjoying the ultimate vertical-jigging presentation the first time they try this tactic.

Tournament professional and river specialist Keith Kavajecz is recognized as one of the nation's leading vertical-jigging experts. A long-time "river rat," Kavajecz cut his teeth fishing for walleyes and sauger on the Mississippi River near Red Wing, Minnesota. Kavajecz discovered quickly that catching river fish re-

Keith Kavajecz is one of the best river fishermen in the nation. Kavajecz grew up fishing the Mississippi River and developing the vertical-jigging method known as "chasing the line."

quires some very specific angling equipment.

"Chasing the line requires a set of tools just like building a house or any other project," says Kavajecz. "An electric motor is the best way to position the boat over the top of the jig. Gasoline kicker motors will also work; however, the most efficient system is a powerful 24-volt, bow-mounted electric motor. The boat's bow is much easier to pull through the water while chasing the line than the boat's transom."

Maintaining boat control and keeping the jig directly beneath the boat is the key to this technique. However, even with a perfect presentation, many fish will be missed if the angler uses rods that feature a slow or soft action.

"The spinning rods most fishermen own are designed to be functional for a wide range of angling presentations," says Kavajecz.

Effectively Fishing Rivers

"A nice flexible rod may look great when it's bending from the weight of a fish, but few river walleyes will be hooked with these soft action sticks."

Kavajecz favors a fairly short (5'6" to 5'9") spinning rod with a rigid medium or medium-heavy action. "Sensitivity in a fishing rod is directly proportional to stiffness," he says. "The stiffer the rod, the better. It can telegraph bites or the feel of the jig ticking along bottom. Soft or slow action rods act like a shock absorber, robbing the angler of important feel and the ability to set the hook quickly with authority."

A No. 10 treble-hook stinger is Kavajecz's next secret weapon. Kavajecz doesn't fish with the ordinary stinger-hook systems available at most tackle shops. Instead, he prefers a specialized stinger using longer and lighter lengths of monofilament line.

"For a stinger hook to do the best possible job, it must be positioned as far back as possible on the minnow," he says. "Most stingers aren't long enough to reach the tail of the minnow. Also, the average stinger is tied using heavy 20- to 25-pound-test monofilament. Short and rigid stingers have the negative effect of reducing natural minnow movement or action."

In comparison, slightly longer stingers enable the angler to position the hook farther back on the minnow. Using 8- or 10-pound-test monofilament on the stinger hook allows the minnow to move around naturally.

Jigging with a thin-diameter, 4-, 6- or 8-pound-test monofilament line makes it possible to keep ⅛- or ¼-ounce jigs directly beneath the boat in swift or deep water. Heavier line creates too much drag in the water, making it extremely difficult to keep it perfectly vertical.

"Chasing the line" combines boat control, stiff action rods, light line, light jigs and stinger hooks into a highly efficient and productive vertical-jigging system.

Wing-Dam Tactics

Many large river systems, such as the Mississippi and Missouri Rivers, are lined with wing dams. Built by the U.S. Army Corps of Engineers, these finger-like appendages are actually linear rock piles that stretch from the shore out into the main current. Strategically placed, wing dams are designed to increase current speed through the main shipping channel.

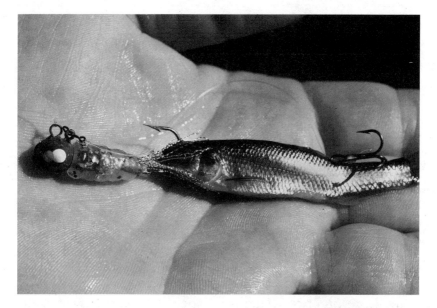

The simple jig-and-minnow combination is the most common bait used by river walleye fishermen. An added stinger hook helps turn short strikes into landed fish. Those who refuse to fish stingers are losing fish.

Water striking these dams is deflected toward the middle of the river, increasing current speed and, in turn, forcing the river to carry its heavy load of sediment downstream. Wing dams help reduce or eliminate expensive dredging operations and keep shipping traffic moving smoothly.

Locating wing dams is easy. Many river maps clearly mark the location of productive fishing dams. Also, water rushing over the top of these linear rock piles causes an easily noticed boil on the surface. Any good fishing graph will also mark these structures as the boat passes over them. Anglers should be careful when navigating over the top of these dams. Some are covered by enough water to allow fishing boat traffic to move freely over them while others are prop-busting demons. It's safer to avoid running your boat directly over the top of wing dams.

Although wing dams weren't built with anglers in mind, they do provide a unique mini-habitat for many species of fish, including walleyes, sauger, smallmouth bass, white bass and catfish. Most fish found around a wing dam will be along the dam's front face near where the rocks forming the dam meet the river bottom. Known as the apex, this small slack-water area is formed when the river current collides with the dam face and is then diverted over and along the side.

Directly downstream from the dams, rolling, turbulent waters create a deep hole referred to as the "scour hole." Walleyes and other fish sometimes can be found in the scour hole, but these fish often are inactive and difficult to tempt into biting. The more active fish will usually be near the apex, or scattered along the front face and top of the wing dam.

Water levels and current speed dictate the walleyes' exact location. In high or swift water, the fish usually tuck in close to bank where the current is a little slower. Small back eddies usually form tight along shore, providing ideal ambush locations for walleyes.

When the water level is normal, the fish spread out along the front face of the dam. Breaks in the dam or debris lodged against the rocks often concentrate these fish.

During extremely low-water periods, walleyes and sauger move toward the tip of the wing dam where the river is swifter and slightly deeper. Extremely active fish can also be found on top of the dam during normal and low-water periods. Casting a diving-style crankbait and retrieving the lure over the top or along the face of a wing dam is often an exciting and productive way to tempt active biters.

It's difficult to describe the perfect fish-holding wing dam. Most river experts agree that certain characteristics reveal whether a particular dam or series of dams will consistently hold fish. Wing dams located along outside river bends often attract excellent numbers of walleyes. This is because these bends naturally concentrate baitfish. If four or more dams are positioned along the bend, the action will be great. Several dams in close proximity deflect and reduce the current more than a single dam, creating an even better environment for baitfish and gamefish alike. The best wing dams in the series are usually those that are situated in the middle.

New dams that aren't laden with silt offer more cover for baitfish and, in turn, attract more walleyes. Also, long wing dams and dams that feature elbow-like bends can be top producers. Bends, breaks or other physical features along the wing dam concentrate fish.

Understandably, anglers who ferret out the best producing dams often are reluctant to share their findings with others. Still,

Complete Angler's Library

certain dams become popular "community" fishing sites. Unfortunately, these popular dams are often poor producers because of the greater fishing pressure.

Successfully fishing wing dams is a challenging and sometimes difficult walleye-angling technique. Positioning a fishing lure along the front face of a wing dam requires extreme boat control. The angler who snoozes for even a moment loses. A steady flowing current can quickly sweep a boat downstream from the dam without the angler even knowing it!

Current near a wing dam is faster and acts like a powerful vacuum, sucking the boat over the dam and out of the fishing zone. Though there are several ways of fishing wing dams, most successful anglers position their boats upstream of the dam. Using a powerful electric motor or small gasoline outboard "kicker" to hold the boat in the current, they slowly slip back and forth along the face of the wing dam.

Keeping the boat's bow pointed into the current when backtrolling along the face of a wing dam is a lesson in futility. Strong currents colliding with the transom make boat control difficult.

A heavy leadhead jig or a Wolf River (three-way swivel) rig are the standard terminal setups for this type of fishing. Jigs are normally used in low to normal current, but a heavy, pencil-style sinker on a three-way rig works well in stronger current. A 24- to 60-inch snell with a single hook, spinner, floating jig head or shallow diving crankbait is normally attached to the three-way rig.

In some states, where it's legal to fish two hooks on one line, the Dubuque rig, a modified version of the Wolf River rig, is a popular river-fishing system. A large leadhead jig is substituted for the bell sinker or pencil weight on a Wolf River rig, allowing the angler a little fish-hooking advantage. Dubuque rigs are not legal in all states so consult local fishing regulations before using them.

Both jigging and rigging systems are baited with minnows, nightcrawlers or leeches, depending upon the availability of bait and the fish's interest. Minnows normally work best early and late in the year while 'crawlers and leeches are preferred for warmer weather.

"I feel strongly about bulking up my presentation with various plastic grub or action tail-bodies," says Stan Berry. Berry and his partner, Harry Stiles, teamed up to win the Masters Walleye Circuit World Walleye Championships.

World walleye champion Stan Berry shows his son the importance of bulking up a jig for river fishing. Adding colorful, plastic tails to a jig makes the overall presentation larger and easier for walleyes to find in murky river water.

Complete Angler's Library

"Bulking up a jig or single hook with plastic grub tails makes the overall lure larger and easier for walleyes to spot," explains Berry. "Plastic bodies also come in a rainbow of colors that help walleyes isolate bait in stained, dirty or off-color waters."

When fishing wing dams, the bait, grub body or terminal rig is usually less important than the accuracy of the lure presentation. Positioning a boat in front of a wing dam and dropping back downstream until a jig or three-way rig contacts the wing dam's apex is no easy task.

Unless the angler pays close attention to his boat-control chores, the lures will be washed up into the broken rock along the face of the dam where they are sure to snag. Lures positioned too far in front of the apex will be out of the primary strike zone, producing very few fish.

Successful anglers cautiously drop their lures back until they can feel the sinkers hitting the rocks at the face of the wing dam. Once the baits are in position at the apex, the boat is moved perpendicular to the current, and the lures are dragged along the face of the dam.

The technique sounds easy, but in reality it requires practice and patience to master. Expect to snag and lose a lot of tackle. Even a skilled wing-dam fisherman snags up frequently. If you don't snag up once in a while, your lures probably aren't close enough to the apex to tempt waiting walleyes.

Most anglers use an abrasion-resistant, 8- to 12-pound-test monofilament to keep the number of break-offs minimal. Both spinning and baitcasting tackle work for fishing wing dams.

Using a stiff action rod makes it easier to detect light strikes, because heavy weights are often used to keep the bait on the bottom. For thousands of anglers, finding and catching walleyes in rivers is the name of the game. Flowing water has much to offer the walleye angler.

=16=

Structure Trolling
And Crankbaits

S tructure and crankbaits are two topics that are seldom discussed in the same walleye-fishing conversation. Ask a group of walleye fishermen the best way to fish structure. Half will say live-bait rigs; the other half will argue that jigging, slip-bobber rigging or drifting bottom bouncers is the way to go.

Structure trolling isn't exactly a new addition to the walleye fishing scene. Like jigging spoons, structure trolling has been around forever; however, only recently have the masses come to acknowledge and practice this technique. It is practiced in many areas and many different ways. Both electric motors and gasoline engines are used to propel the boat. Some anglers troll forward, while others backtroll.

A large percentage of the fish taken are caught in natural lakes and reservoirs. The traditional (obvious) spots see some angling pressure. Main lake points, sunken bars, mid-lake reefs and a lot of man-made structure receive varying degrees of angling pressure.

Many times, man-made structure, such as rubble-covered banks, break walls, pier heads, sea walls and even artificial spawning reefs provide the necessary bottom cover and structure to attract walleyes. The fishing may take place during the day, but the "night bite" is more likely to produce greater numbers, as well as larger fish.

Surprisingly, major river systems also yield excellent crankbaiting potential. Perhaps the most commonly overlooked walleye-

Trolling cranks is an excellent way to cover water quickly while hunting for walleyes. Once a walleye is located near particular structure, other presentations can be applied to completely work over the area.

Structure Trolling And Crankbaits   165

fishing opportunity, structure-trolling cranks in rivers has much to offer the minority of anglers who practice this technique. Structure trolling is a complex and exciting way to fish walleyes.

Gasoline Vs. Electric Power

The great debate continues almost every time a gasoline troller passes an angler trolling with an electric motor. Those who prefer gasoline trolling motors scoff at electrics. The common complaint is that electric motors are not powerful enough to handle serious trolling chores.

On the flip side, fans of electric motors claim that the churning growl of a gasoline motor, even small kicker motors, spook walleyes away from the boat and ultimately the trailing lures.

In reality, a bit of truth exists in both complaints. Electric motors can be marginal trolling tools in windy conditions or if the angler chooses an electric motor too small for the job. Gasoline motors probably spook a few fish, especially in clear, shallow or very calm waters. However, when the winds pick up, a small gasoline motor may be the only feasible option. Ironically, these types of fishing conditions often provide the best structure-trolling bite.

The latest generation of electric motors offers trollers considerably more thrust and extended service life. For serious structure trolling, a 24-volt electric motor is essential. The sustained power of a 24-volt system makes short work of most trolling situations. Under normal conditions, electric motors provide more than enough power to troll all day or night.

Both 24-volt transom- and bow-mounted electric motors are available. Bow-mounted electrics are an advantage if the angler primarily trolls forward.

From the bow, boat control becomes a snap. Positioning the boat along a breakline or contour is easy as the motor pulls the boat along. In comparison, it's somewhat difficult to push a boat forward with a transom-mounted electric motor. When wind and wave action cause the bow to drift off course, boat control becomes more difficult.

A transom-mounted motor is recommended for backtrolling situations. For fishing winding contours, backtrolling offers the most precise boat control.

Some serious structure trollers rig their boats with both bow-

The author poses with an early-season walleye that smacked an oversized crankbait pulled along a rocky shoreline. An electric motor was used to avoid spooking fish.

and transom-mounted electric motors. Depending upon fishing conditions, the angler then can choose the better motor position for the job. A variable speed control and a constant "on" switch enable the angler to fine-tune and set boat speed for consistent trolling results.

Select an electric motor with a little more power than necessary. A motor that has more than enough power for average conditions will shine when the weather turns nasty and fishing effectively requires a little extra thrust.

Many small, gasoline kicker motors are available. The 8-, 9.9- or 15-horsepower models are the most popular with walleye fishermen. Each provides plenty of power for all structure-trolling situations. The larger, horsepower-rated engines cost more; however, they provide a "kick" to move larger boats.

Structure Trolling And Crankbaits

Structure trolling can also be accomplished with larger 20-, 25-, 30-, 40-, 50- and even 75-horsepower engines. Unfortunately, many of the larger motors will not idle slow enough for some trolling situations.

Which Bite, Day Or Night?

Many anglers argue over the ideal trolling motor; others disagree on the best times to structure troll. An effective presentation, trolling crankbaits over bottom structure has no limit during the day or after dark.

Most anglers would agree that walleyes bite better early and late in the day. However, these same fish are just as likely to bite during the middle of the day, if the environmental conditions are right.

Wind and wave action influence feeding times for walleyes more than the time of day. When the wind whips the surface into a chop, the chop reduces the amount of light that is penetrating the surface.

Low-light levels favor walleyes that see best in dim light, while baitfish that see best in bright conditions are at a disadvantage. Naturally, walleyes quickly take advantage of any opportunities when it comes to finding an easy meal.

Certain bodies of water offer either a better day or night bite. In general, fisheries featuring very clear waters often produce a dismal daylight bite. Fishing after dark is often the only way to effectively approach walleyes in clear water.

Bodies of water with significant boat traffic are also prime candidates for night-fishing. Ski boats, jet skis and other recreational crafts often churn up the waters of popular fishing lakes and rivers like a blender mixing daiquiris. On the most popular waters, only at night does the lake activity calm down enough to allow walleyes and other predatory fish to feed undisturbed.

Even fisheries providing dependable, daylight trolling bites often yield better fishing once the sun sets. Walleyes are opportunistic feeders. Under the cover of darkness, these predators go on the prowl. With their oversized eyes, walleyes can see many species of baitfish that can't see them after dark.

This is why walleyes are normally more active early and late in the day. Low-light hunting conditions favor the walleye. Despite the fact that walleyes are less wary and easier to catch after dark,

Structure trolling after dark is one of the best ways to tempt trophy-class walleyes into biting. Mike McClelland poses with an 8-pound-plus walleye he trolled up from Lake Erie. After posing for a quick photo, the fish returned to the water to fight another night.

Structure Trolling And Crankbaits

however, very few anglers fish the graveyard shift.

A lake, river or reservoir, familiar as your backyard, suddenly becomes an intimidating place after dark. Developing confidence in night-fishing takes some time. Like any activity, practice makes perfect. This is especially true when fishing in the dark. Even minor tasks become amazingly difficult.

Most dedicated night trollers outfit their boats with battery-operated lamps that provide enough light to accomplish basic tasks, such as tying on lures or sharpening hooks. Black lights illuminate the immediate work area; yet they aren't so bright that nearby fish are warned of approaching danger.

Choose Your Weapon

Crankbaits are the weapons of choice for structure trollers. Although other lures could certainly be trolled with some degree of success, cranks are the only logical choice. Aimed at a specific depth zone like a hunter would aim a gun, lipped or floating/diving-style crankbaits offer the angler a wide array of depth ranges, actions and profiles.

Diving depth is a major concern for those who troll crankbaits. Common sense suggests that the reason for structure trolling crankbaits is to position the lure close to the bottom without actually hammering the bait into it. Ironically, pounding the bait into the bottom is one of the most effective presentations.

A crankbait smashing into, and bouncing off of, rocks or other bottom debris has a strong triggering effect on walleyes. Apparently the lure bouncing off objects and darting off at unpredictable angles sends a message to walleyes that are hunting for an easy meal.

Unfortunately, the life expectancy of a crankbait fished this way isn't long. Snags and lost lures are an inevitable problem. Also, the angler who fishes hard will eventually wear out his lures.

Most structure trollers attempt to present their cranks within 12 inches of the bottom. At times, especially after dark, walleyes suspend several feet over structure that they would normally hold tight to. Anglers should watch their electronics carefully for signs of suspended fish. Walleyes suspending over structure are the most active and easily caught fish. As soon as suspended fish are spotted on the graph, you should adjust the diving depth of the crankbaits accordingly.

This walleye struggles to toss the crankbait it mistook for something good to eat. Trolling crankbaits over bottom structure or cover is one of the least practiced yet most effective ways to catch walleyes.

Three basic elements influence crankbait-diving depth: size of the lure's diving lip, line diameter and lead length. Crankbaits with a large diving lip will dive deeper than those with a smaller lip. Unfortunately, all big-lipped baits don't reach the same maximum depth ranges. The lure's body size and natural buoyancy also influence maximum diving depth. Line diameter and lead length are less obvious influences, yet extremely important. An angler using 10-pound-test line for trolling will find his lures dive considerably deeper than another angler fishing the same lures on 14-pound test. The larger the line diameter, the more resistance there is in the water. Lighter lines allow crankbaits to reach their maximum possible depth ranges.

Most structure trollers depend upon 10-, 12- or 14-pound test for walleye fishing. With light lines, there is the risk of loosing valuable lures, but running heavier line seriously reduces the diving depth range of crankbaits.

An abrasion-resistant, low-stretch monofilament line works best because banging lures along the bottom calls for a tough monofilament fishing line. Lines with a low-stretch rate enable the angler to feel lure action and light bites better, and not lose hooksetting power.

Anglers need to pay more attention to lead length. In general, the longer the lead, the deeper a lure will run. Even though there is a point of diminishing return, lead lengths should be monitored so successful lead lengths can be accurately replicated.

Fishing reels with digital line counters are the most convenient means of metering lead length. Simple to use, a counter keeps track of the number of feet of line that is let off the spool. The convenience of using line-counter reels has a price: They are nearly double the price of regular trolling reels.

Metered fishing lines having a color band every 10 feet are a handy tool for monitoring leads. These color bands are an easy, accurate and affordable means of keeping track of lead lengths. The only drawback is that color-coded bands are difficult to see in dim light.

Many anglers solve this problem by measuring out predetermined amounts of line before going onto the water. A broken strip of rubber-band knot is tied into a firm knot on the line and the tag-ends clipped short enough so the rubber band can slide easily through the rod guides and onto the reel.

When setting lines, it's easy to spot the rubber bands. Even in total darkness the angler can feel the knots bumping their way through the rod guides.

Until recently, the only way to determine how deep a crankbait will dive is to tie one on and troll it. The old trial-and-error method of determining crankbait diving depth separates the men from the boys in a big hurry. Only those anglers willing to experiment, take notes and work hard knew how deep their lures ran.

It was walleye professional Mike McClelland who first opened the door to structure trolling crankbaits. McClelland spent months researching the diving depths of various lures on common line sizes, and then published the data in a book. The data were confirmed on a paper graph that actually recorded the depth diving curve and maximum depth of over 200 crankbaits. For the first time, anglers were offered accurate information on exactly how deep their lures were running. A trolling lead of 120 feet was used for developing the data. When the lead length is changed, the diving depth of these lures also changed.

This is only the tip of the iceberg as far as structure trolling is concerned. So many possible combinations of lead lengths, trolling speeds, crankbait models and other variables exist that it's unlikely a single publication could answer all the questions.

In addition, many structure trollers add one or more split shots on the line about 3 to 5 feet in front of their lures. Though a tiny split shot may not seem like much weight, the depth gained by split-shot-weighted lures is significant.

Perhaps one day soon on-board computers will help anglers program the exact lead length, added weight and lure needed to achieve perfect depth control. It would probably take a computer memory just to store all the possible combinations.

In the meantime, those who aren't afraid of doing things the hard way are learning the best possible fishing methods. The information an angler discovers through hours of experimenting on the water is extremely valuable.

=17=

Open-Water Trolling

Trolling for suspended walleyes is not an art; it's a learned science! The science of trolling can be described as a means of reproducing various fishing variables in order to catch walleyes. Reproducibility is a term coined by one of the nation's leading experts on open-water walleye trolling. Gary Parsons has been fishing open-water walleyes since his father gave him his first rod and reel. Born and raised along the shores of Lake Winnebago in central Wisconsin, Parsons learned the effectiveness of trolling at an early age.

The Evolution Of Crankbait Trolling

Long before the invention of the planer board, anglers trolled crankbaits on long leads known as flatlines. Setting the lures 100 or more feet behind the boat helped the lures reach maximum diving depths. More importantly, the boat had passed through the school of walleyes long before the lure arrived.

A spooky fish by nature, suspended walleyes are especially adverse to having boats pass directly above them. By using long leads, anglers could give the fish a chance to settle down and mill around before the crankbaits were among them.

Planers, or skis as they are often called, revolutionized trolling and added another dimension to a technique thousands of anglers consider their No. 1 walleye-producing method.

The first fishing skis resembled a snow or water ski. Made from lengths of buoyant wood, such as cedar and pine, these early

Gary Parsons is credited with popularizing the use of in-line planer boards for walleye fishing. A walleye fishing pioneer, Parsons has developed many effective trolling patterns.

Open-Water Trolling

boards worked despite their crude design. Most were made from 1-by-6 lumber, roughly 3 to 6 feet long.

An eye bolt was attached to the front of the ski where a tether line could be tied in place. While the boat moved slowly forward, the tether line was fed out and the board tracked off to the side of the boat.

Early skis also had a second eye bolt attached to the back of the ski as well. A length of fishing line with a crankbait attached was tied to it. No fishing rods were used with these early planers; instead, the ski was pulled in periodically and the line checked to see if a fish was hooked. If a fish was on the line, it was brought in hand-over-hand. Then, the lure was let out once again with the line firmly attached to the back of the ski. Crude by today's standards, this labor-intensive form of fishing paved the way for a wealth of modern planer boards.

Today, two major types of planer boards dominate the walleye-trolling scene. The first is by far the most popular and widespread. Known as catamaran boards, two wooden or plastic boards are attached side by side. Using two boards helps the skis track to the side better and run more smoothly in rough waters.

One end of a tether line is attached to the front of the ski and the other is connected to a line-retrieval spool and planer mast mounted near the front of the boat. The planer mast keeps the tether line elevated and prevents it from dragging in the water. The retrieval spool is a convenient way of letting out or taking in the board and prevents the tether line from getting tangled.

Using rigging lines on catamaran-style boards requires specially designed line releases. Designed with various spring tensions, most releases operate the same: A spring holds the line firmly between two rubber or plastic pads. The release is attached to the fishing line and then clipped over the tether line where it is allowed to work its way out toward the ski.

When a fish strikes the crankbait, the line is pulled free of the release mechanism so the angler finds himself fighting only the fish—not the board, extra weights or other trolling gear.

Catamaran-style boards are an effective trolling system and are popular with charter captains who operate large boats, because a number of lines can be run on either side of the boat. These boards continue to gain in popularity wherever suspended walleyes are sought and caught; however, they do have a few disadvantages which should be given careful consideration.

Cost is one disadvantage. Two double boards, a planer mast, retrieval system, tether line and an assortment of line releases will cost between $200 and $400, depending upon the brand. Also, catamaran boards work better at fairly fast trolling speeds. For best results, an average trolling speed of 2 to 3.5 miles per hour is required. At slow speeds, the boards don't track properly and the tether lines may drag in the water. At that point, crisp line releases are all but impossible.

Catamaran-style boards are most effective in producing walleyes during the summer months when the fish are active and aggressively feeding. At other times, cold-blooded walleyes can be difficult to catch on crankbaits unless you can reduce the trolling speed to a snail's pace.

Because of these and other reasons, some anglers have switched to the smaller, in-line planer boards which attach directly to the fishing line by a line-release system connected to the board. No additional releases, tether lines, retrieval systems or planer masts are required.

Advantages of the in-line planer board include its reasonable cost. Average cost is $10 to $30 per board. Trolling speed is another advantage that these mini-skis offer. Because the boards are smaller and don't need tether lines, the in-line skis function well at all common trolling speeds, but probably work best in the slower speed ranges. For early- and late-season fishing, slow-trolling crankbaits behind in-line boards is becoming a preferred method for producing trophy-class walleyes.

Another consideration is that in-line boards also increase lure action. Wave action tosses these boards around like a tiny skiff in a gale-force blow. Small and lightweight, in-line boards speed up and slow down as they climb and crest the waves. This causes the crankbaits to be constantly darting forward and hesitating for a few seconds. This erratic action helps trigger strikes from fish that might otherwise remain unimpressed.

One walleye tournament professional deserves credit for helping the in-line board achieve its popularity. Gary Parsons has been fishing in-line boards for more than 10 years. During that time, he has successfully used side planers to win several walleye tournaments and catch thousands of fish.

Parsons' winning trolling tactics aren't complicated, they're

Trolling with in-line planer boards is easy to learn and an effective way to catch suspended walleyes. During summer months, trolling crankbaits behind planer boards produces many walleyes.

efficient. "Catching suspended walleyes is as easy as 1, 2, 3," says Parsons. "It all boils down to three simple steps. First find the fish; second experiment until the fish tell you what they're biting on; and third duplicate what's working."

Finding the fish may seem difficult, but, actually, suspended walleyes are often easy to locate. "Concentrate the search on large sand, clay or mudflats that average 20 to 50 feet deep," suggests Parsons. "Suspended walleyes are usually located on large flats that attract huge numbers of baitfish."

If the graph isn't marking baitfish or walleyes, keep moving until suspended fish start appearing. "It doesn't take a lot of marks to interest me," says Parsons. "Remember, electronics only scan a small portion of the underwater environment. A few marks directly beneath the boat could possibly indicate hundreds of fish in the area."

Once fish are located, in-line planers play a major part in Parsons' open-water trolling techniques. "Side planers provide two important functions," he says. "First, they significantly increase my trolling coverage. Instead of fishing a narrow path behind the boat, in-line boards enable me to sweep lures through a tremendous amount of water quickly and efficiently. Secondly, the boards act as strike indicators when a fish is hooked."

Increasing the trolling coverage is the first step toward finding suspended walleyes. Parsons normally fishes two boards on each side of the boat or a total of four lines. On calm days, the outside boards may be run 100 to 125 feet from the boat. Inside boards are usually 30 to 40 feet closer.

Each line offers a different crankbait and lead length combination at the start of each fishing day. "My goal is to cover as many depth ranges as possible when I first begin trolling," says Parsons. "Even though I may be marking a large school of fish at 20 feet, I'll usually set one line to run much shallower and one a little deeper than the main school."

Many times, active and easily caught walleyes are suspended well above the main school. These fish are often so close to the surface that the graph rarely shows them. The only way to find them is to fish for them.

Large adult walleyes, however, often position themselves just beneath the main school. From this vantage point, the larger fish can pick off dead or dying baitfish missed by the more aggressive members of the school.

"Running at least one bait below the main school has helped

Open-Water Trolling

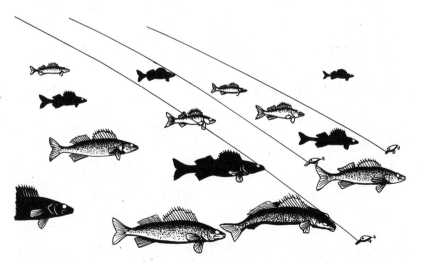

In the typical school of suspended walleyes, the larger fish are often found slightly deeper than the rest of the school. Apply your presentation accordingly when open-water trolling.

me hang a number of trophy-class walleyes," says Parsons. "The bigger fish frequently form loose groups and position themselves somewhere below the main school. Find this school within a school and you can do some serious damage in a hurry."

Rigging and setting in-line boards is easy. As for other forms of trolling, the lure first must be set a desired distance behind the boat. The lead lengths chosen help to determine how deep the crankbait will run. In general, the longer the lead, the deeper the bait will dive. However, other factors, including line diameter and lure type, also affect crankbait diving depths.

A firm release tension prevents the board from accidentally popping free; the board should remain on the line until the angler removes it. The board can now be placed in the water and it will track out from the side of the boat. Only two lines normally run on each side of the boat to minimize tangles.

With four planers set and running properly, the boat begins sweeping a huge chunk of water. The boards position themselves alongside the boat in a symmetrical pattern resembling an airplane squadron.

When a walleye is hooked, the fish's weight pulls the in-line planer backward out of formation. Spotting hooked fish is simple. With a little practice, detecting strikes becomes second nature.

Fighting a hooked fish is also a simple process. Reel in the board with a smooth, steady retrieve. "There's no need to jerk on the rod or set the hook," says Parsons. "As long as steady pressure is applied to the fish, few will shake the hook."

When the board comes within reach of the boat, remove it and fight the fish as before. Keep the boat moving forward while reeling—the forward motion of the boat helps eliminate slack in the line. Once the board is removed, the boat can be slowed (or even put in neutral) until the fish is landed. This gives the angler more control during the fight.

After landing the fish, kick the motor in gear, reset the lure behind the boat, attach the board and continue fishing.

Monitoring details like lead length can make a big difference in trolling success. Using a line-counter-style fishing reel is the easiest way to meter lead length, but using color-coded fishing line with different colors at 10-foot intervals is easy and inexpensive, too. Duplicating a successful lead length enables the angler to return his lure to the exact depth range. Once this valuable infor-

These anglers watch as their planer boards track out to the side. When a walleye strikes and becomes hooked, the board will pull backward in the water. With a little practice, even novice anglers can use crankbaits and in-line boards to effectively harvest suspended walleyes.

Open-Water Trolling

mation is determined, it's a simple task to adjust unproductive lines accordingly.

Choose Your Weapon

Parsons uses numerous crankbait shapes, styles and colors to do the job. "Don't get hung up on one favorite bait," he says. "A hot bait today is just as likely to be useless tomorrow. I experiment a lot, changing lures frequently until the fish tell me which ones they prefer on any given day."

Experimenting with different cranks is the best way to get familiar with the type of action each bait offers. Studying lure action is important because certain action-types seem to work better than others, depending upon trolling conditions.

"Crankbaits can be divided into three basic categories," says Parsons. "High-action, medium-action and low-action baits all have a time and place when trolling for open-water walleyes. Early and late in the year when the water is cool, I've found that low- or medium-action baits trolled at slow speeds produce best. During midsummer when the water is warm and the fish aggressive, a high-action bait produces the most bites."

Unfortunately, an angler can't look at a bait in the box and tell if it has a high, medium or low amount of action. Studying various baits in the water is the best way to determine each bait's action category.

Wobblers with their violent back-and-forth movement are high-action baits that have large and wide diving bills; a snake-like, back-and-forth movement in the water characterizes high-action baits. In comparison, medium-action lures often feature a narrow bill and a minnow- or shad-shaped body.

Moderate- or medium-action lures exhibit a little wobble combined with a pronounced side-to-side roll. The crankbait's roll can be described as a vertical wobble. Instead of moving aggressively back and forth, rollers quiver from side to side. Not all medium-action lures fit the shad- or minnow-shaped body description. The best way to identify medium-action lures is to pull them alongside the boat, watching closely to see how they move in water.

Low-action baits are easy to recognize. Usually minnow-shaped, these baits have small diving lips and slender bodies. Often referred to as stickbaits, low-action lures have very little action at all. A slight wobble and roll typify these baits.

"Knowing when to use high-, medium- or low-action baits is often the key to trolling success," says Parsons. "I concentrate on fishing lures that closely match the mood I suspect the fish to be in. In other words, if the fish are active, an aggressive high-action bait will probably work best. Neutral fish might require a medium-action lure and cold water or lethargic walleyes are sure to hit low- or subtle-action cranks over all others."

No official guidelines have been developed for running crankbaits, but common sense goes a long way. In the summertime when the water is warm and the fish active, all three bait categories are likely to produce fish. As summer stretches into fall, lures with more subdued actions dominate the scene. In extremely cold water, nothing beats a subtle-action stickbait.

Successful crankbait trolling for walleyes is just like putting together a jigsaw puzzle: Piece by piece, the pattern takes shape.

18

Salmon Tactics
For Walleyes

Walleyes are suckers (excuse the pun) for a trolling tactic designed to catch king, coho, pink and Atlantic salmon. Much of what the salmon pros have learned about catching kings and cohos is just as effective on a smaller but no less important Great Lakes-area gamefish. The deep and clear waters of Lake Erie, Lake Huron and Lake Michigan, as well as Lake St. Clair, are a perfect setting to test taking walleyes with salmon-fishing tactics.

It's been known for many years that walleyes will suspend to feed on shad and other suspended (pelagic) forage fishes. What wasn't common knowledge is that these fish frequent depths that are more attuned to lake trout than depths most anglers consider normal for walleyes. Catching walleyes far below the surface is a job best accomplished with downriggers.

Understanding Downriggers

Downriggers are a common sight on salmon boats; however, few anglers understand how effective these trolling aids can be for catching walleyes. Downriggers allow anglers to present lures at much greater depths than they can with traditional walleye-fishing tackle.

Commonly associated with deep water, 'riggers provide more than a means of fishing far below the surface. Downriggers also serve as depth-control aids because a lure can be accurately presented at any depth down to 100 feet or more.

Big walleyes come deep. This torpedo-shaped trophy took a shallow-diving crankbait trolled 100 feet behind a downrigger weight positioned 4 feet off the bottom in 60 feet of water. Fish that measure 28 to 32 inches in length are frequent rewards of downrigger fishing.

Salmon Tactics For Walleyes

Despite the fact that 'riggers are seldom used in shallow water, the depth control these trolling aids provide offers the angler an almost endless list of presentation options regardless of the depth. Various lures, including spoons, crankbaits and even live-bait spinner rigs, produce walleyes when fished in combination with downriggers. Of course, making the successful transition from salmon to walleyes requires a few adjustments in attitude, equipment and angling savvy.

The Speed Debate

Trolling speed is the chief difference between fishing for salmon and walleyes. The average salmon angler moves along at twice the speed considered normal for walleye trolling.

Learning to slow things down is the first and most important hurdle for a walleye-fishing newcomer. The fact that salmon and walleyes feed differently is the chief reason successful trolling speeds for the two species differ so radically.

Salmon are powerful swimmers, built to attack open-water prey. Salmon will slash into a school of baitfish like sharks during a feeding frenzy. Trolling speeds averaging 3 and even 4 mph are common among salmon trollers.

Walleyes, by comparison, are not physically equipped to chase fast-moving baitfish in open water. More timid predators, walleyes instinctively understand that feeding on easily caught, injured, sick or dying forage fish provides maximum protein return with minimal amount of expended energy.

Rapid trolling speeds result in catching only the most aggressive walleyes. Slowing down the boat's forward progress extends the amount of time a lure remains in the strike zone and provides walleyes with a more tempting target.

How slow is slow? The average walleye trolling speed falls around 2 mph. Keeping in mind that speed is a relative term, one angler's idea of slow may seem too fast to the next troller.

Wise trollers experiment constantly with speed. Early and late in the year when water temperatures are cold, slower trolling speeds produce best. During the summer, when walleyes are most active, a brisk trolling pace will often yield the best results.

Some anglers claim that super-slow trolling speeds are the hot ticket. Don Parsons, a retired Wisconsin contractor, has spent a lifetime trolling for walleyes at speeds akin to a snail's pace.

Downrigging Lures

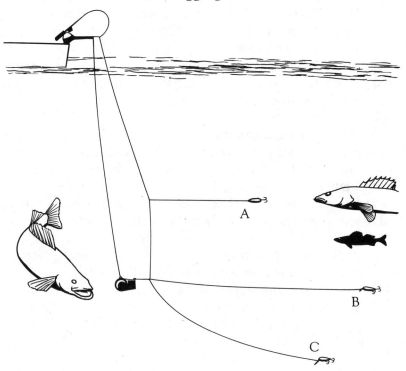

Various lures, including flutter spoons (A), shallow-diving crankbaits (B) and deep-diving crankbaits (C), can be used effectively with downriggers. Walleye fishermen should experiment with different methods to increase their walleye-catching success.

"Trolling for walleyes is a numbers game," he says. "Slow trolling keeps you in the school of fish longer and increases the odds of contacting and catching more fish per pass."

Parsons noticed early in his trolling career that boats moving quickly through a school of walleyes usually would pick off one or two fish before the trolled lures had traveled through the school. "Trolling one mile per hour or less keeps my lures in fish twice as long," says Parsons. "By doing nothing more than trolling slower, I often catch two or three times as many walleyes from the same group of fish."

Downrigging And Terminal Tackle

Spoons are among the most popular downrigger trolling lures. Flutter-type spoons are preferred over casting models. Thin and lightweight, these lures provide more action and flash when trolled at normal speeds than heavier spoons do. Spoon trolling is popular with downrigger fishermen because these lures run at exactly the same depth level as the 'rigger weight. Maintaining depth control is never a problem when fishing spoons. These simple fish attractors also work well at various speeds and are much easier to unhook from struggling fish and landing nets than multihooked crankbaits.

A typical, walleye-trolling presentation consists of a flashy flutter spoon attached to a dependable snap swivel. The swivel helps prevent the spoon from twisting the line into hopeless snarls.

Available in sizes ranging from mini to magnum, spoon size is often relative to walleye size. Fishermen seeking trophy-sized walleyes find that magnum salmon spoons produce the best results. Fishing with large spoons has the unfortunate effect of reducing or eliminating normal-sized fish from the catch. A spoon 3 inches long is the most popular all-around lure among walleye trollers.

Where legal, many anglers add a second spoon attached to a 6- to 8-foot leader a few feet above the downrigger weight. This little rigging trick, known as the stacker, allows the angler to simultaneously fish two different lures at different depths on one fishing line.

A stacker is a piece of monofilament leader with a snap swivel at each end. A lure is attached to one swivel while the other swivel is clipped on the main line before the downrigger ball is lowered. A rubber band is half-hitched over the main line to hold the stacker in place.

A stacker can be placed anywhere along the main line; however, most anglers set stackers 5 to 10 feet above the downrigger weight. When it is hooked on the stacker, the struggling fish pulls the snubbed leader along the main line until the snap on the stacker pulls tight against the lure on the main line.

Don't be intimidated by this technique. It takes longer to describe a stacker than to rig and set one. Just be sure to check local fishing regulations before using stackers.

Question Of Lead Length

A short lead length, 10 to 20 feet, is considered normal for trolling spoons. Placing the spoon a short distance behind the downrigger weight increases lure action. Longer leads tend to reduce spoon action. Still, many anglers think longer leads are more effective despite the fact that there is less lure action.

A growing number of anglers think that downrigger weights and the hum from wire cable moving through the water spook walleyes. Although no one knows for sure if these foreign materials and sounds in the water spook fish, running longer leads is an easy way of reducing the negative impact that downrigger hardware might have on fish.

Anglers report excellent results from using short leads in murky waters. In clear water, however, leads averaging 20 to 50 feet are often more productive. Tempting reluctant walleyes, especially fish affected by cold fronts, may require 50- to 100-foot leads.

Determining the best lead length is a trial-and-error process. Experimenting with long and short leads helps anglers determine the best possible lead for a particular day on the water. The type of lures used also influence the best possible lead lengths. And, NAFC Members shouldn't feel that lure choice is limited to spoons. Many shallow- and deep-diving crankbaits also are ideal candidates for downrigger trolling for walleyes.

Crankbaits offer downrigger trollers the widest selection. Just about any shape or size crankbait can be fished off of downriggers. Shallow, medium and deep divers all have their time and place.

The diving characteristics of crankbaits make them an especially useful tool for this kind of trolling. The downrigger weight can be run above the school of walleyes while the crankbait dives down into the unsuspecting school of fish.

In order to achieve maximum diving depths with crankbaits, the angler must use longer lead lengths than those used with spoons or spinners. In general, the longer the lead length, the deeper the crankbait will dive.

The most common leads range from 50 to 75 feet. At times, exceptionally long leads of 100 to 150 feet are needed for the lure to attain its maximum diving depth or to tempt spooky fish. It's important to keep a record of lead lengths. Lead length helps determine the diving depth of crankbaits, so it's important that the angler monitor and duplicate successful leads.

Downriggers And Live Bait

Few anglers associate downrigging with live-bait fishing. Bait rigs, such as nightcrawler harnesses and cut bait, are also an effec-

Trolling deep-diving crankbaits with downriggers has enabled anglers to catch walleyes at amazing depths. In Lake Erie and other Great Lakes fisheries, walleyes are often caught 50 to 75 feet beneath the surface. In some cases, walleyes have been reported as deep as 120 feet.

tive option for downrigging. Like spoons, live-bait rigs will maintain the same depth as the downrigger weight. The ordinary nightcrawler harness is a walleye killer when it's fished off of downriggers.

Many spinner-blade styles, sizes and colors interest walleyes. As stated earlier, Colorado- and Indiana-style blades are the most popular, but many anglers swear by French-style blades.

A slow trolling speed is necessary for trolling spinners or cut bait. Trolling at brisk speeds with these baits only cause annoying line twists. However, attaching an in-line barrel or ball-bearing swivel will help eliminate some of the line twist.

Getting The Most From 'Riggers

For a downrigger trolling system to work properly, the lure

must be set behind the downrigger ball and the line must be attached to the ball by some sort of line-release system. In theory, the line-release mechanism will trip when a fish strikes, and the angler can fight the fish without having to raise the downrigger weight.

This release system works great with salmon and other large fish. Unfortunately, walleyes aren't as big as salmon, so even above-average walleyes often are unable to pop the line free. Therefore, the angler needs to check the lines often because a hooked walleye could be dragged along without the angler even knowing it was on.

If long trolling leads are used, line stretch contributes to the walleye's inability to trigger the line release. In other words, getting walleyes to trip the trigger is a losing battle.

Ironically, many walleye trollers have discovered that the best downrigger release system is one that doesn't release at all! A firm-tension release that holds the line until the angler snaps the rod upward sharply is usually best. This manual release method allows the angler to trigger the release and take up slack line all in one smooth motion.

A firm-tension release puts the angler in control of the situation. When a strike is detected, the angler should sweep the rod upward in a strong swift movement. Snapping the rod upward pops the release and pulls the line taunt against the fish. Few fish are lost because line slack is kept to a minimum. A strong rod sweep also helps to set the hooks solidly.

While the "no release" rigging system is effective, the angler must somehow know that a walleye has been hooked. Walleye trollers aren't clairvoyant, so a technique allowing some type of rod movement as a tip-off was developed.

The answer was a handful of rubber bands. Once the lead length for the lure is determined, a No. 16 rubber band is half-hitched over the line at that point and pulled tight. The rubber band is then inserted into a pinch-pad-style trolling release and the downrigger weight lowered to the desired depth.

As the downrigger ball sinks, the angler lets out line while keeping a steady light pressure on the reel spool. When the weight is at the correct depth, the angler engages the reel and reels up any slack line until the rod has a gentle bend in it. This pulls the rubber band upward at a slight angle.

No-Release Rigging With Rubber Bands

The no-release rigging system consists of downrigger, rod, monofilament line, wire cable, cannon ball weight, pinch-pad release and half-hitched rubber band. When a fish is hooked, the rubber band bends, allowing rod to bend. This signals the angler to remove rod and set hook hard, breaking or releasing rubber band. The angler is then in direct contact with fish.

The give in the rubber band allows the rod to bounce and jiggle. The hooked walleye pulls against the rubber band causing the rodtip to bounce in such a way that tips off the observant angler.

All the angler needs to do is remove the rod from its holder and sweep the rod upward sharply. That sweep pulls the rubber band free and the angler is in direct contact with the fish.

It takes a little practice to detect a bite this way. To the untrained eye, the rodtip will seem to be bouncing because of the wave action and the boat's natural movement. To a more trained eye, however, the rhythmic movement of the rodtip as a result of wave action or boat motion differs noticeably from the rod movement produced by a strike. Developing an "eye" for spotting these subtle but important rod movements comes with experience.

Obviously keeping a close watch for rodtip movement is critical. It doesn't hurt to check lines frequently, however. It's pretty easy to detect strikes on flat, calm days, but when the waves start rolling, it's difficult to read the rodtip effectively.

=19=

Winter Walleyes Under Ice

Contrary to popular belief, the walleye-fishing season doesn't end when the winter solstice begins. Even though ice and near-freezing water temperatures put the brakes on fish activity, winter angling can be surprisingly effective. The arrival of cold weather, snow and ice signals a dramatic change in walleye-fishing tactics. With a couple notable exceptions, most species of gamefish become lethargic and more difficult to catch during the winter months.

Research indicates that northern pike, for example, remain active all winter long, and large specimens may actually be more active in winter's frigid waters than during the dog days of summer. Another unique sportfish, the burbot, actually spawns under the winter ice.

Despite these unique exceptions, most other fish, including walleyes, go into a semi-dormancy stage during the winter months. Walleyes and other fish don't stop feeding all together. Because their metabolism rate has slowed considerably, however, the amount of food required in order for them to survive is significantly reduced.

In other words, when a walleye gobbles down a perch in February, it may take a week or more for the walleye to digest the meal. The same meal in July might only last a couple of days before the predator is forced to eat again.

During the winter, walleyes aren't finicky about what they eat; however, they are forced to feed efficiently because of their slug-

The average walleye taken through the ice weighs a pound or two more than one taken during the open-water period. Two-pounders like this make nice winter sport and are perfect tablefare.

Winter Walleyes Under Ice   195

gish nature and the general scarcity of forage. Seldom will a winter walleye travel a long way in search of food. Every movement uses up valuable energy and fat reserves that will be needed when the spring spawning season arrives.

Limited by the temperature of their environment and their metabolism's reaction to it, walleyes become lethargic by design, not choice. Feeding periods are shorter and less predictable than during the rest of the year.

This window of angling opportunity—when winter walleyes are feeding—may only last for 10 to 15 minutes once or twice a day. So, it's easy to see why limit catches of winter walleyes are rare even in waters that hold an abundance of catchable fish.

The First Step: Finding Fish

Ice fishing for walleyes is truly a challenge for even the most savvy angler. Locating and catching a fish that seems to evaporate at will help build the walleye-fishing mystique. It is a labor-intensive operation. Designed for angling from a boat, modern fishing electronics can't effectively show depth changes or mark fish unless you have cut a hole through the ice first.

Consequently, locating walleye structure is basically a trial-and-error process. Lake maps and shoreline sightings can help the angler find the general area, but pinpointing fish-producing spots usually requires cutting a lot of holes.

The process might be an impossible chore if it weren't for the army of anglers all trying to achieve the same goal. Collectively, these groups of fishermen help to unlock the winter mystery of walleye location. Fortunately, fishermen are gregarious, and there always seems to be room for one more angler. Tight clusters of anglers on the ice are a common sight on popular walleye-fishing lakes.

The shanty towns that "pop up" on productive spots are a welcome sight and serve as an ideal starting point. Your search may start and stop at the first cluster of shelters. But, finding a crowd on the ice doesn't guarantee good fishing.

Crowds suggest that either a bite is going on or has taken place recently. Savvy ice anglers seldom pass any collection of shanties without stopping to fish for a few minutes. Watch for other anglers who are fighting fish. Being observant is often more valuable than having a fish locator.

When looking for a walleye ice-fishing location, pay attention to clusters of shelters on the ice. Usually, several shelters mean walleyes are biting in the area.

Clusters of anglers make it easier to locate potential hotspots; but noise, confusion and fishing pressure are also part of the package. Commotion on the ice, including grinding power augers, screaming snowmobiles and pounding spuds, frequently put a premature end to an otherwise productive bite.

Sometimes it pays to work the edges of a crowd. Staying close to productive areas, yet keeping unnecessary noise levels away makes sense. It also makes sense to drill a series of 10 or more holes spaced 20 to 50 yards apart. Once the last hole is augered, return to the first hole and begin fishing. Letting things quiet down for even a few minutes before testing each hole can make a big difference in your success rate.

Also, moving frequently helps increase the odds of contacting fish. The most successful anglers spend a maximum of 10 to 20 minutes at each unproductive hole before moving. Finding the fish is the real secret to successful winter-walleye fishing.

Terminal Tackle

Fishermen wouldn't be fishermen if they weren't in the market for a lure or bait that's guaranteed to improve fishing success. Human nature makes them suckers for flashy lures, marketing claims and gadgets that promise the world. Rarely does the lure brand or, for that matter, the type of lure make much difference when you're winter-walleye fishing.

A 10-cent leadhead jig tipped with a minnow will most likely catch just as many fish as a jigging lure or spoon that costs $3 to $5. Nothing is likely to prevent anglers from stocking their tackle boxes with scores of winter-fishing lures. The truth is, however, that the type of lure is insignificant during the winter.

Finding fish that are in a feeding mood is much more important than trying to force-feed walleyes a certain brand of lures. A modest assortment of three different lure groups is sufficient for the winter-walleye angler. These groups include leadhead jigs, jigging/swimming lures and jigging spoons.

Simple and effective, the leadhead jig tipped with a minnow has probably been a more successful walleye producer than all other lures combined. Although available in many different shapes, sizes and colors, a small selection of 1/8-, 1/4- and 1/2-ounce jig heads and a few colorful plastic grub bodies are a good place to start. Most anglers probably could round up enough change from seat cushions, coat pockets and the bottom of the washing machine to purchase an impressive and effective assortment. Anglers should also invest in a few stinger hooks. Adding a stinger hook to any jig-and-minnow combination—where it's legal—will significantly increase the number of walleye bites.

Jigging/swimming lures are to winter-walleye fishing what crankbaits are to summer trolling. Designed to imitate a darting and confused minnow, these lures are horizontal at rest and swim forward when jigged. Between jigging strokes, these lures glide back into a horizontal position. Although effective winter-walleye producers, most jigging/swimming lures seem to have two faults. The hooks on these lures are usually too small to be dependable for hooking success. Also, jigging lures usually feature single hooks extending from both ends of the lure that usually catch on the

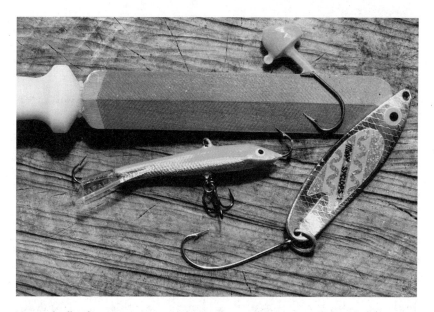

Various leadhead jigs, jigging spoons and jigging lures are all the winter-walleye hound needs to catch fish. Maintaining sharp hooks is extremely important in winter months; light-biting fish are often difficult to hook and hold.

ice's surface while the fish is being landed. Replacing the treble hook with one a couple sizes larger will cure the first fault and increase the number of solidly hooked fish. However, keep in mind that countless numbers of walleyes have regained their freedom because one of the single hooks snagged on the ice at the least opportune moment.

Anglers can choose from several brands, sizes and colors of jigging/swimming lures. Although the price range varies and is fairly high, most jigging/swimming lures are similar in style and are designed to accomplish the same basic function.

Jigging or slab-style spoons make up the third important group of winter-fishing lures. Dozens of manufacturers produce countless models of vertical-jigging spoons.

Variations in shape result in different fluttering-type actions and rates of fall. The width and thickness of the spoon primarily determine how fast it will fall through the water. Wide and rather thin spoons usually have the slowest drop time and the most aggressive wobbling action. Narrow spoons sink quickly and provide the least amount of fluttering action.

Spoons also come in many different finishes that add color and flash to a live-bait presentation. Those models featuring highly polished finishes, hammered surfaces and colorful flash tape are often the best producers.

Spoons are probably the most popular all-around, winter-walleye lures, although jigs and jigging/swimming lures will often out-produce spoons. However, it's difficult to beat a lure that offers the appeal of live bait combined with both flash and action like the spoon does.

Rods, Reels, Line

A winter-walleye angler needs to be concerned about the quality of his rod, reel and line. Notoriously light-biters, winter walleyes seldom engulf a lure with the type of enthusiasm that summertime anglers expect. Rod sensitivity, or the ability to feel subtle bites, becomes critical.

In recent years, the quality and availability of commercially built ice-fishing rods have skyrocketed. Extremely high-quality graphite, graphite/fiberglass composite and fiberglass ice-fishing rods can be bought for less money than it would cost to build your own rod.

The ideal winter-jigging rod ranges in length from 24 to 36 inches. Whether the rod will be used inside an ice house or on open ice is an important consideration when choosing for length. Short rods are handy for use inside an ice shack while longer rods provide a little extra control when fighting large fish in the open.

Most anglers prefer to use spinning-style rods matched with ultra-light spinning reels that usually have been modified slightly for use in extremely cold weather. The gears of most spinning reels are packed by the manufacturer with a heavy petroleum-based grease that can stiffen in cold weather. To prevent the reel from freezing up, some anglers replace the existing lubricant with a polymer-style grease that's impervious to temperature.

Fishing line is a frequently overlooked subject among ice fishermen. At no other time of year is the quality of monofilament more important. Freezing temperatures cause fishing line to stiffen, resist stretching and break more easily than the same line in warmer conditions.

During summer, most walleye anglers settle on 6-pound test as the best all-around diameter fishing line. Winter angling is an entirely different matter.

A compromise between limpness and strength must be made. The line must be limp enough to offer maximum action to jigging lures, yet strong enough to resist breaking in frigid temperatures.

Eight-pound test is an all-around good choice for winter-walleye fishing, especially if there is a chance of catching larger-sized fish. When the average fish taken will weigh less than 3 pounds, 6-pound test is adequate.

Mobility And Shelter

Just as sensitivity in winter jigging rods is important, mobility can be critical to winter-jigging success. Being able to move about freely on the ice and cover large amounts of water efficiently is more important than the lures used to tempt walleyes.

A snowmobile, quad runner or other all-terrain vehicle is perhaps the best investment in angling success that a winter-walleye fisherman can make. An ice-fishing vehicle and some type of sled or cart to haul necessary gear are "must have" items for serious winter fishing.

Power augers also can help transform ice fishing from hard work into a labor of love. Capable of cutting through 2 feet of solid ice in just a few seconds, a power auger enables winter fishermen to drill countless holes in one day. (Few anglers would have the energy to carve dozens of holes with a hand auger or ice chisel.)

Modern outdoor clothing is warmer, drier and more comfortable than anything our grandfathers ever imagined. Still, being exposed to freezing temperatures for hours on end takes its toll. A portable shelter, or shanty, enables anglers to wait out winter walleyes in comfort.

All sorts of models from simple three-sided, canvas windbreaks to elaborate portable ice houses that can be towed with a snowmobile or ATV are available. The amount of money an angler is willing to spend is about the only limiting factor.

It takes more than body heat to warm an ice house. Portable heaters can turn winter into summer inside. Radiant-style propane heaters are popular because they are lightweight, compact and easy to use. Many models come equipped with automatic ignition systems, eliminating the need for matches.

Summing It Up

Although winter-fishing equipment and clothing are much

A power auger is essential for serious winter-walleye fishing. Ice fishing is a numbers game: The more holes you drill a day, the better your odds of locating fish.

better today than they were just a few years ago, the sport of ice fishing is a demanding hobby. Those who trek across the ice in hopes of finding fast action and limit catches are heading toward disappointment.

The appeal of ice fishing lies more in the hunt than the capture. Winter-walleye anglers work harder for less return than just about any other group of fishermen. Despite the extra work, freezing temperatures and smaller catches, you'll rarely hear anyone complaining.

Interest in ice fishing continues to grow, even though most anglers know that the number of bites per day will most likely be low. Watching these anglers battle the elements provides a renewed faith in human nature.

Where And When

20

Heartland Walleyes

Minnesota, Wisconsin and Iowa are indeed the pulse of walleye fishing. Every weekend hundreds of pick-up trucks, vans and suburbans pulling deep "V" boats flood the highways and waterways of these states in pursuit of their favorite sportfish—the walleye. Heartland walleye fishermen are some of the most dedicated and serious anglers in the country.

Consider some of the respected professional anglers who have lived in this region. Big-name walleye fishermen Gary Roach, Al Lindner, Babe Winkelman, Gary Parsons, Mike McClelland, Keith Kavajecz, Daryl Christensen and Art Lehrman got their start in the walleye heartland.

In addition, many of the nation's fishing tackle and marine manufacturers are or have been based in this region: Berkley, Lindy Little Joe, Northland Tackle, Bait Rigs, Jig-A-Whopper, St. Croix, Lund, Mercury, Mariner, Johnson and many others.

Some of the best walleye fishing anywhere is within this three-state radius. Walleye, sauger and saugeye are plentiful in most lakes, reservoirs and rivers throughout this region.

Lake Mille Lacs
Lake Mille Lacs is one of the best known Minnesota walleye factories, and the most complex. Numerous fishing presentations produce walleyes on this 115,000-acre pond, depending upon the time of year.

206   Complete Angler's Library

Gary Roach poses with a better-than-average-sized Lake Mille Lacs walleye. Special harvest regulations, including slot limits and closed seasons during the spawning period, have helped Lake Mille Lacs remain one of the finest walleye fisheries despite heavy fishing pressure.

Heartland Walleyes

Known best for producing large numbers of average-sized walleyes, Mille Lacs is also capable of producing the occasional trophy-class walleye. Carefully planned fishing regulations have helped preserve this fishery, despite enormous fishing pressure and a walleye sportfishing harvest that usually dwarfs the production of most lakes.

Fisheries biologists use slot limits to control the harvest of mature, breeding-sized walleyes. Anglers are allowed to harvest several small (under 20 inches) walleyes, but only one large fish over the legal slot-size limit may be taken per day. Placing a slot limit on the fishery prevents anglers from inadvertently harvesting too many adult spawners and helps spread the sport harvest over the most abundant portion of the total population.

However, slot limits are just one of the ways biologists manage this unique fishery. Maintaining a closed season during the spawning period and setting a minimum size limit of 15 inches have also helped Mille Lacs grow into a world-class fishery.

Everything from jigging to pulling crankbaits with planer boards produces fish on Mille Lacs. Slip-sinker rigging on the sand at the north end of the lake is popular in early spring. In June, many anglers power-troll spinner rigs tipped with nightcrawlers on mid-lake mudflats. During the summer months, crankbaits trolled as flatlines or behind planer boards take many suspended walleyes.

When the wind increases, many walleye anglers will use slip bobbers and leeches to harvest limit catches from the many shallow rock reefs.

Anglers enjoy a consistent open-water fishery from mid-May to October. During the winter, thousands of anglers take up residence in the ice shacks that dot the entire lake. Perhaps the best winter-walleye fishery in the nation, Mille Lacs yields more walleyes through the ice than most lakes generate all year long.

Big Stone Lake

Located on the Minnesota/South Dakota border, Big Stone Lake rates high as a walleye fishery. A shallow body of water, Big Stone may have the highest walleye-per-acre ratio of any lake in the heartland.

Huge walleye schools, with fish ranging from 14 to 16 inches in length, roam the lake and are easily caught by anglers trolling

Who says rivers don't grow trophy wall-eyes? This lunker was taken by Dan Roach on the Mississippi River near the town of Red Wing, Minnesota. Known primarily for yielding small saugers, this fishery produces a number of trophy walleyes each year.

crankbaits and spinners. An excellent population of large adult fish is also present. Casting jigs and crankbaits to shoreline structure produces the best catches of adult fish. Many of the best fish are found in extremely shallow water.

Mississippi River At Red Wing

The Mississippi River near Red Wing, Minnesota, is one of the most productive stretches of walleye water anywhere in the country. A flowing well of walleye and sauger action, the water from the dam downstream to the town of Red Wing produces outstanding response to jigging action from late winter through spring.

A leadhead jig tipped with a small fathead minnow is standard fare. Stinger hooks are mandatory when the bite slows.

The fishery is dominated by 1- to 2-pound sauger; however, many walleyes and good numbers of jumbo-sized sauger are also taken. A respectable number of walleyes over 10 pounds are taken in early spring. Sauger approaching 4 pounds can be caught, but 2- to 3-pounders are more the norm.

Lake Pepin

Approximately 10 miles downstream from Red Wing, a wide spot in the Mississippi River, known as Lake Pepin, produces excellent summer and fall walleye/sauger catches. Anglers are allowed to fish this boundary water with proof of either a valid Minnesota or Wisconsin license.

Most of the fish are taken on jigs and rigs that are tipped with 'crawlers or minnows and fished along the channel breaks and main lake points. In the summer, 'crawlers and small minnows work best. In early September, the bite has usually switched over to minnows. As the water gets colder, larger-sized minnows produce the best action. Small suckers and redtail chubs are local favorites when they are fished slow on a jig or slip-sinker rig.

A growing number of Lake Pepin anglers troll small crankbaits weighted down with lead-core line. A 10- to 15-foot monofilament leader is attached by a blood knot to the lead-core line. The crankbait attaches to the monofilament leader and various amounts of lead-core line are let out until the crankbait can be felt hitting bottom. Small minnow- or shad-shaped crankbaits are the most popular.

Those who troll with lead core often concentrate on large flats; however, the technique is equally effective along channel breaks, rocky shorelines and other structure.

Mississippi River In Iowa

Three pools along the Mississippi River attract a lot of attention from heartland walleye anglers. The Guttenberg, Dubuque and Bellevue pools offer excellent river cross-section fishing opportunities. Normally the river is a year-round fishery—only the most bitter winter weather puts a halt to the fishing action. (Anglers fishing these boundary waters need an Iowa, Wisconsin or Illinois fishing license.)

In late fall, winter and early spring, most fish can be found near the head of the pools. The spillway, adjoining tailrace and riprap banks offer jig anglers an excellent proving ground. After the spring spawning run, the fish disperse downstream and take up residence along the main-river channel, sunken rock piles and the many wing dams protruding from shore.

During high-water periods, the fish move in close to the bank and often inhabit many backwater sloughs and lakes scattered along the river's edge. As water levels return to normal, walleyes and sauger move back into their normal river haunts.

Of the three pools, the Guttenberg pool receives the least fish-

These anglers wait patiently while the water level in the lock and dam reaches the level of the upper pool. Lock-and-dam systems are common on the Mississippi River in Minnesota, Wisconsin and Iowa waters. Anglers who want to fish more than one pool per day may lock upstream or downstream at the lockmaster's convenience.

ing pressure and produces some of the most consistent walleye and sauger catches. The Dubuque pool receives heavy fishing pressure. Despite the many anglers plying the waters near the city of Dubuque, this pool continues to provide good to excellent walleye-fishing opportunities.

The Bellevue pool also suffers from heavy angling pressure, as well as intense pleasure-boat traffic on warm summer days. Anglers are often forced to fish either early or late in the day to avoid the masses of water skiers, jet boaters and pleasure cruisers.

Wing dams in the Guttenberg pool near the town of Cassville, Wisconsin, are popular fishing sites. Hurricane Chute and the region near Mud Lake are also consistent walleye/sauger producing regions.

Those anglers who fish wing dams depend heavily on three-way sinker rigs baited with leeches, 'crawlers or minnows. Most anglers add a plastic grub body or action tail to increase their presentation's action and bulk. A jig-and-minnow or jig-and-crawler combination is tops when the fish move into the backwaters or along channel edges.

St. Croix River In Wisconsin

Wisconsin's St. Croix River is a sleeper walleye factory. A

tributary of the Mississippi River, the St. Croix drains into the mighty Mississippi just above the town of Red Wing, Minnesota. Known for its spring, summer and fall sauger bite, the St. Croix also harbors an excellent walleye population in the 2- to 5-pound range. Most of the fish are taken on jigs fished along the channel edges and off protruding points. In the spring, minnows are the preferred live bait. The warmer summer months see a bait switch to 'crawlers and leeches, with minnows working best in September and throughout the winter.

A few local guides do well during the summer months by trolling crankbaits on lead-core line. The combination of diving cranks and lead-core line is used to dredge up walleyes and sauger from the deeper main channel. Better-than-average-sized fish are taken with regularity by those who know the river.

Lake Winnebago System

The Lake Winnebago system is Wisconsin's largest walleye/sauger producing watershed. Comprised of Lake Winnebago, Lake Poygan, Lake Butte Morts, and the Fox and Wolf Rivers, this region has a long and rich walleye-fishing history.

Although this region has seen brighter fishing days in past years, the lakes and adjoining river systems continue to maintain a self-sustaining population of walleye and sauger. A unique strain of marsh-spawning walleyes exists in Lake Winnebago. Early each spring, walleyes leave Lake Winnebago to make spawning runs into the Fox and Wolf Rivers. Instead of seeking out rock and rubble areas to spawn, the Lake Winnebago walleye strain chooses to spawn along marshy shores of flooded soft maple and willow.

After spawning, the fish begin returning to Lake Winnebago. Along the way, anglers intercept the fish in Lakes Poygan and Butte Morts. Both lakes are shallow, mud-bottom basins that support heavy aquatic weed growth.

Anglers using crankbaits and planer boards troll the open waters, catching 2- to 5-pound walleyes. Emergent cane beds similar to cattail stands also attract large numbers of post-spawn walleyes. Anglers fish the cane by poling their boats quietly through the thick grass and dibbling a jig tipped with a leech into pockets of open water. These shallow-water walleyes are tackle-busters when hooked in the cane.

Walleyes are also taken in rivers connecting Lakes Poygan and

Butte Morts to Lake Winnebago. Jigging vertically with minnows is a common method for tempting the roaming schools.

By early June, most of the fish have returned to Lake Winnebago. Open-water and structure-trolling presentations produce walleyes and sauger, or what the locals refer to as "sand pike." In-line and catamaran-style planer boards are a common sight on Lake Winnebago all summer long.

Approximately 20 miles long, Lake Winnebago has the potential to be a world-class walleye fishery. The naturally produced population of walleyes has declined seriously in recent years, however. Poor spawning year classes combined with heavy sport-fishing harvests have brought this once-great fishery to its knees.

A sometimes-heated dispute between local anglers and the Wisconsin Department of Natural Resources leaves little hope that this fishery will rebound in the near future. The state refuses to stock walleyes in the Winnebago system, arguing that subsequent interbreeding could destroy the native stocks of marsh-spawning walleyes. Local fishing clubs maintain that supplemental stocking would help get the fishery back on its feet and pour needed recreation and tourism dollars into the region.

The Lake Winnebago region produces some of the best walleye fishermen in the country. More than half the anglers who qualify to fish the two major walleye-fishing championships have come from this central Wisconsin region.

Summing It Up

The heartland of walleye fishing in this country continues to grow and expand. As the nucleus gets stronger, the excitement spreads to more and more distant communities.

Everyone who enjoys the tug of a nice fish owes something to the heartland anglers who, through the years, have standardized and popularized walleye-fishing methods in this country.

Heartland anglers got the ball rolling and provided the energy to make walleye fishing one of the fastest-growing sportfishing activities in America.

=21=

Great Lakes Area Walleyes

H arboring the fastest-growing populations of walleyes in North America, the Great Lakes offer the best walleye-angling opportunities available anywhere. Lake Erie, Lake St. Clair, Saginaw Bay, Little Bay de Noc and many other areas that are within the Great Lakes Region have much to offer the walleye-fishing fanatic. The explosion of walleye-fishing opportunities in this region has not gone unnoticed. Each year the number of nonresident angling licenses sold increases dramatically.

Lake Erie

An enormous body of water, Lake Erie boasts hundreds of miles of shoreline, touching the shores of Michigan, Ohio, Pennsylvania, New York and Ontario.

Lake Erie, like many other Great Lakes fisheries, has a few skeletons in the closet. Many anglers remember the days when Lake Erie was considered to be a dead sea. Industrial and agricultural pollution almost cost the country one of the finest fishing waters in the world. Fortunately, the pollution problems Lake Erie once faced are in the past. The vastly improved water quality of Lake Erie currently supports the largest concentration of walleyes found anywhere in the world. Individual schools of fish, numbering in the tens of thousands, make this fishery stand alone.

From a fisherman's perspective, Lake Erie is divided into three sections, or basins. Michigan, Ohio and Ontario waters primarily

Lake Erie, which produces walleyes like this, is divided into three major regions: the Western Basin, Central Basin and Eastern Basin. Fish migrate from the Eastern Basin in late fall and continue until the fish spawn in late April or May in the Western Basin. After spawning, the fish gradually move east and north searching for baitfish schools.

Great Lakes Area Walleyes

make up the Western Basin. Farther east, Ohio, Pennsylvania and Ontario waters are referred to as the Central Basin, and the boundary waters of New York and Ontario encompass the Eastern Basin.

The Western Basin consists primarily of shallow water filled with countless rock reefs, shoals and islands. Literally millions of walleyes cram into the extreme west end of the lake during spawning season. Some of the fish migrate into river systems including the Maumee, Raisin, Sandusky and Detroit. Even more fish remain in the lake to spawn on the countless rock reefs, gravel shoals and rocky shorelines.

Almost immediately after spawning, an eastward migration of fish begins. Spawned-out fish follow the prevailing winds that push plankton and baitfish east toward the Central Basin. The migration process is obvious, but it takes time for so many fish to leave one region of the lake.

Spawning is usually complete by early May, but the Western Basin continues to hold fish through May and June. By early July most of the fish have migrated to the Central Basin. The migration doesn't stop. July and August find most of the fish in the Eastern Basin, hundreds of miles from where they spawned in April.

During the fall, the migration route is reversed, and walleyes begin a long westward trek to the headwaters of Lake Erie. The Bass Islands, located in Ohio waters, seem to hold the largest concentration of late-fall and winter walleyes. As soon as the ice melts in spring, many fish migrate into spawning streams; others remain in deep water, staged near spawning reefs.

Angling strategies vary greatly on Lake Erie, depending upon season and location. In the relatively shallow Western Basin, spring anglers begin casting or vertical jigging for walleyes using leadhead jigs and slab-style spoons.

After the spawn, hordes of anglers begin using a regionally unique lure known as the weight-forward spinner. A combination of a jig and in-line spinner, weight-forwards are normally baited with a glob of nightcrawlers and retrieved just fast enough to keep the spinner blade rotating.

Drifting and casting are the most common means of fishing weight-forwards. Simply dragging the spinner along the bottom is productive on bottom-hugging walleyes. Fish that are suspended off bottom are taken with a countdown presentation. With this method, the spinner is allowed to sink to the proper depth before being slowly retrieved.

A spinner sinks about one foot per second. Counting the seconds before starting the retrieve enables the angler to control the lure's depth.

As the waters continue to warm, suspended walleyes become more prevalent. Trolling crankbaits is an important late-spring and summer angling strategy. Planer boards are used to position diving crankbaits 75 to 100 feet from the sides of the boat. Spreading out a trolling pattern using planer boards increases the amount of lure coverage and helps catch fish that might otherwise be spooked by the boat's presence.

Significantly deeper waters, the Central and Eastern Basins are primarily trolling fisheries. Throughout the Eastern Basin, mixed catches of walleyes, steelhead, lake trout and salmon are quite common. In fact, salmon tactics produce the majority of the walleyes landed in this region. Deep-water trolling gear, including downriggers, wire line and diving planes, produces best in these clear waters.

The Niagara River also is a growing walleye fishery. A sleeper among Great Lakes rivers, the Niagara receives a good to excellent run of spring and fall walleyes. Jigging with spoons, leadhead jigs and weighted blade baits produce the best action.

Lake St. Clair

Although not officially one of the Great Lakes, Lake St. Clair connects to Lake Huron by the St. Clair River on the north and Lake Erie by the Detroit River on the south. A shallow body of water, Lake St. Clair is known best for drift fishing—a unique fishing method that many anglers use on its waters.

Unlike Lake Erie anglers, Lake St. Clair anglers have no allegiance to the weight-forward spinner. The shallow waters of this inland sea produce a bumper crop of aquatic weeds, and dense weed cover provides an excellent environment for walleyes. However, it also makes it difficult to fish with traditional methods, such as trolling crankbaits or drifting bottom rigs.

Excellent catches of Lake St. Clair walleyes are taken by anglers who drift the garden-variety nightcrawler harness over the tops of submergent weed growth. A small split shot or two is added to the line about 3 feet ahead of the bait. The weighted lead shot helps sink the 'crawler a few feet below the surface.

Ideally, the crawler should drift along right at the top of submerged weed growth. The amount of weight it takes for the bait to drift effectively changes, depending upon wind conditions and boat drifting speed.

Walleyes that live in dense weed patches aren't shy about rocketing toward the surface to latch onto a spinner-and-nightcrawler combination. In areas where the weeds have defined edges (such as along drop-offs), dragging spinners near bottom is the preferred angling method.

Drift socks, or sea bags as they are often called, are a common sight on this body of water. Anglers use these parachute-like bags to slow down and control drifting speeds.

The fast-flowing waters of the St. Clair River also provide a unique and productive walleye fishery. Strong currents make it difficult to fish with jigs, rigs or other traditional bottom-bumping systems. Instead, area anglers anchor their boats and practice a unique form of crankbait fishing called handlining.

No fishing rods are used in this method. A length of wire line with a heavy sinker is pulled through the water by hand. Enough weight is used so the angler has constant contact with the bottom, even in strong currents. A long, monofilament leader with a thin, minnow-imitating bait, known as a pencil plug, is attached just above the lead weight. In some cases, two or more lures are run off one leader.

While trolling against or with the current, the handliner lets out wire line until he feels the weight hitting the bottom. Wrapping the wire around a gloved hand, the angler simply trolls along slowly, swinging his arm back and forth in a rhythmic motion. The movement of the angler's arm creates lure action.

Excess wire is stored on a special reel that pulls the wire in much the same way an automatic fly reel picks up fly line. When a fish is hooked, the angler winds up the wire until the weight reaches the boat. The weight is pulled into the boat and the angler uses the monofilament leader to fight the fish hand-over-hand.

It's crude form of angling by modern standards, but handlining is very popular on the St. Clair and Detroit Rivers. Handlining is certainly unique and also one of the most effective means of harvesting walleyes in the region. A folk art of sorts, the craft typically is practiced after dark.

Michigan-based charter captain Al Lesh shows off a typical Detroit River walleye. The Detroit River receives a massive spring spawning run of walleyes from Lake Erie and nearby Lake St. Clair. Vertical jigging produces many lunkers like this.

Detroit River

Although one of the shortest streams in the country, the Detroit River is one of the richest river fisheries. The connecting link between Lake St. Clair and Lake Erie, this river system serves as a boundary between Michigan and Ontario.

Primarily a shipping route for Great Lakes cargo vessels, the Detroit River also hosts millions of walleyes during the brief spring spawning runs. Walleyes from both Lake Erie and Lake St. Clair converge on the river from March through May to spawn on the rocky shores and among the broken boulders covering the river bottom.

Walleye fishing can be phenomenal during the peak of the spawning run. Jigs tipped with small shiner minnows are the standard bait. Strong river currents can make jigging difficult in some areas. Anglers should seek out side channels and other areas that offer slightly reduced current. The Trenton Channel, located a few miles upstream of Lake Erie, is a popular and productive spot.

The fishing season for walleyes is open year-round on the Detroit River. Hundreds of anglers fish the river every day during the spawning runs. At times, limit catches are the norm—even among novice anglers.

During the peak of the spawn, it's not uncommon for a hooked female to be accompanied to the surface by half a dozen smaller males. Many anglers have been confused and dumbfounded when netting a fish that doesn't have a hook in its mouth!

A limited fall fishery for walleyes also exists on the Detroit River. Late October and November are the best times to find fall action.

Saginaw Bay

The walleye-fishing opportunities of Saginaw Bay in Lake Huron may soon approach those of Lake Erie. Roughly the size of Erie's Western Basin, Saginaw Bay is the fastest growing of all the Great Lakes fisheries.

Saginaw Bay wasn't always a walleye factory. During the 1940s, commercial overharvest and depredation of spawning habitats decimated the native walleye strain in Saginaw Bay. Eventually, commercial fishing was banned. It took nearly 30 years to successfully reintroduce walleyes into Saginaw Bay.

A number of efforts to stock walleye fry failed. It wasn't until 1978 that the first successful plants of walleye fingerlings started the Saginaw Bay fishery back on its way to recovery.

In just 10 years, the walleye population in Saginaw Bay skyrocketed as a result of an ambitious stocking schedule of nearly one million fingerlings per year.

Fueled by an almost limitless forage base of shad, alewives, smelt and emerald shiners, Saginaw Bay walleyes grew to maturity in just three years. Lack of predation from other fish and commercial and sportfishing pressure has also helped the population expand at an amazing rate.

Today, Saginaw Bay has one of the strongest walleye sportfisheries in the nation. The annual sport harvest exceeds 300,000 fish and continues to climb each year.

With the bay open to year-round sportfishing, anglers are just

With its aggressive stocking, Saginaw Bay may soon rival Lake Erie as the No. 1 Great Lakes walleye fishery. Saginaw Bay fishing experts Gary Parsons and Keith Kavajecz bring another trophy fish to net. This fishing team dominates tournaments held on this body of water.

Great Lakes Area Walleyes

221

beginning to learn how to catch these fish throughout the calendar year. Primarily a spring and summer fishery, Saginaw Bay also hosts excellent ice-fishing opportunities when conditions allow—the bay doesn't freeze over every year. During many winters this huge body of water is open in all but the worst of weather.

Much of the spring fishing takes place close to shore. River mouths feeding nutrient-rich water into Saginaw Bay attract huge numbers of baitfish and walleyes from April through June. Major tributaries, including the Saginaw and Kawkawlin Rivers, are popular fishing locations.

Main lake points, small bars, reefs and sand flats are likely places to look for action. Anglers drifting, casting or using electric motors to slow-troll live-bait rigs dominate the fishing scene during the spring months. Most fish are caught in 4 to 10 feet of water until late June when excellent catches of walleyes start coming far from shore. Hordes of suspended shad, alewives and smelt attract walleyes in enormous schools.

Trolling crankbaits on planer boards is the most popular angling technique throughout the summer months. In recent years, a fleet of charter boats equipped to travel far off shore and catch these open-water fish has developed on the bay.

Trolling success improves as the summer progresses. The end of August typically offers some of the best fishing of the year.

As the trolling bite begins to level off and decline in early fall, so does angling interest. Although Saginaw Bay has great potential as a fall walleye fishery, few anglers take advantage of this resource.

Trolling for suspended walleyes dominates the summer fishing scene on Saginaw Bay; however, keep in mind that the same areas producing fish in spring also have excellent numbers of walleyes all summer long.

Lake Michigan/The Bays de Noc

Located in Michigan's Upper Peninsula, Little Bay de Noc is actually an appendage of Lake Michigan. Once considered to be a world-class walleye fishery, Little Bay de Noc suffered many of the same problems associated with Saginaw Bay in the post World War II days.

A stocking program similar to the one enacted on Saginaw Bay has helped Little Bay de Noc recover its world-class fishing

Little Bay de Noc is one of the smallest yet most impressive Great Lakes fisheries. The region receives strong walleye plants and produces some of the finest trophy walleye fishing available. The author poses with an average Bay de Noc walleye.

status. Up to a half million walleye fingerlings are planted each year in either Little or nearby Big Bay de Noc. One year Little Bay de Noc gets the plants and the next year fingerling plants go into Big Bay.

Both bodies of water offer excellent walleye-fishing opportunities; however, Little Bay de Noc is more accessible and has the heaviest angling pressure. Little is known about Big Bay de Noc in terms of fishing information, although during the spring, anglers find excellent numbers of post-spawn walleyes in the extreme northern part of the bay.

A similar fishing pattern exists in Little Bay de Noc. Spawning streams located in the northeast corner of the bay attract both walleyes and sportsmen in mid-May when the fishing season opens. As the season progresses, the fishing gets better. By late

July or early August, the first schools of suspended walleyes start appearing and anglers are quick to capitalize on them.

Planer boards and crankbaits are a common sight on these waters all summer long. As summer grows into fall, the numbers of fish taken drop off slightly, but the average size starts to increase dramatically.

Known for producing large numbers of trophy-class walleyes, Little Bay de Noc is a hub of trophy-fishing activity during October and November. Anglers catch fish by using a wide variety of tactics. Slow trolling with oversized crankbaits, however, produces many of the biggest fish.

The biggest fish stay close to the bottom in deep water at this time of year. Specialized trolling gear, such as lead-core line and downriggers, is used to present lures tight to the bottom in the 30- to 50-foot range.

Trolling slowly is the key to success. Although these fish willingly bite, fast-moving lures produce few strikes.

Fall walleye fishing remains good until cold weather and ice bring an end to the open-water sport. As soon as the ice layer grows thick enough to support the weight of a man and snowmobile, a winter fishery explodes.

Little Bay de Noc usually freezes solid by December and stays ice-covered until April. Walleye fishing is permitted until the last day of February, then the season is closed to protect fish preparing to spawn.

Miscellaneous Fisheries

The Great Lakes are full of places to catch walleyes. The major locations attract most of the angling pressure. However, many out-of-the-way walleye fisheries provide excellent angling opportunities because few anglers compete for the action.

The mouth of Michigan's AuSable River located along Lake Huron's northern shoreline harbors an excellent fall and early-spring walleye fishery. The months of October and November produce a surprising number of fish over 10 pounds. Every year some lucky angler takes home an AuSable-River walleye that tips the scales at more than 14 pounds!

The harbor town of Oscoda—just north of the AuSable's mouth—is a hub of fishing activity. Anglers troll or cast crankbaits along the riprap and river shoreline, channel edges and pier heads. Jig fishing is also effective in the river. Many fish are taken during the day, but the best action takes place after sunset.

Another Michigan port city produces notable walleye catches. Muskegon once was a busy Great Lakes shipping port. Today, sail boats, yachts and other pleasure boats fill its harbor and its lake.

At night, however, a small fleet of charter boats hits the water in search of trophy-class walleyes. Muskegon Lake, Muskegon Harbor and the connecting shipping channel yield an amazing number of midnight walleyes.

Trolling large stickbait-style plugs and using silent electric motors work best. Good fishing begins in late summer and lasts throughout the fall.

The Great Lakes, their connecting waters and the many tributaries that drain into these enormous inland seas have some of the finest walleye-fishing opportunities in the world. An untapped resource in many respects, walleyes routinely die of old age without ever seeing a fisherman's lure. The trophy potential in these waters is also undisputed. A virtual smorgasbord of forage fish provides walleyes with more than enough nutritional food to grow to trophy proportions.

=22=

Wilderness Walleyes

Beautiful wilderness scenery, clear waters and untapped walleye fisheries are major attractions for any angler. It's easy to understand why so many fishermen travel to Canada in search of a walleye-fishing paradise. Those who cherish the adventure as much as the fishing will discover that Canada offers countless lakes, rivers and reservoirs that seldom see fishing pressure. Even those waters that see a considerable amount of angling efforts are rarely pressured with the latest angling tactics. In short, serious angling pressure is rare across much of the Canadian provinces.

Every year a migration of American anglers heads north to fish the unspoiled waters of Saskatchewan, Manitoba and Ontario. The southern half of these provinces abound with walleye-fishing opportunities that are within a day's drive across North Dakota, Minnesota, Wisconsin, Michigan, Ohio, Pennsylvania, New York or beyond.

A little farther north lies some of the finest walleye fishing available anywhere in North America. Accessible strictly by float plane, the northern-most reaches of Ontario and, to a lesser degree, Manitoba and Saskatchewan provide pristine and productive walleye fisheries.

Although the number of fish harbored in many wilderness lakes is absolutely astonishing, individual growth rate is painstakingly slow. Highly susceptible to angling pressure, walleyes in these wilderness waters provide a delicate fishery that must be

Complete Angler's Library

In Canada, small float planes carry fishermen and their gear to remote northern waters that seldom see modern fishing pressure. Every walleye angler should get the chance to fish Canada's pristine waters.

carefully managed so that there will be quality fisheries for future generations. Harvest restrictions are the most common means used by fisheries managers and lodge owners to preserve breeding stocks.

Many lodges in wilderness country only allow their guests to take home one trophy-class walleye. Smaller fish may be harvested for the table, but the majority of adult fish captured are set free to spawn again. This type of foresight guarantees that Canada's wilderness walleye-fishing opportunities will continue for many generations.

Planning The Drive-In Trip

Those planning to visit the near North have many destination and accommodation options available to them. Lodges ranging

Wilderness Walleyes

from simple tent camps to luxurious five-star resorts are available to fit the constraints of any pocketbook.

Most lodges offer anglers a choice of housekeeping or American-plan lodging packages. Which plan is best depends largely upon the amount of money the angler has to invest and how many "creature comforts" are desired.

Housekeeping plans are the most affordable lodging packages. The basic essentials are provided, including lodging, linen, bedding, cooking utensils and, in most cases, a rental boat. Guests are responsible for doing their own cooking, cleaning and preparation of fish for transportation home. In some cases, for an additional fee, guests can rent an outboard motor, have their fish cleaned and frozen and hire maid service and a fishing guide.

In comparison, the American-plan packages provide a full service vacation. In addition to lodging, maid service and boats, meals, guides and fish-cleaning and freezing services are included. A breakfast and supper meal are normally planned for designated times each day. Either a box lunch or a shorelunch prepared by the guide is often provided as a noon meal.

(Some of the better lodges provide a daily boat cleaning service, wake-up service with morning coffee and even someone to stoke up a fire in the wood burner on those chilly mornings.)

Having ready-made meals waiting each morning and evening is an advantage for anglers who want to spend more time on the water. Some anglers avoid the added cost of American-plan meals by designating a member of the fishing party to handle cooking and cleaning chores each day. The designated cook for the day is responsible for getting up before the other anglers and preparing breakfast and box lunches. Once everyone has eaten breakfast, packed away a box lunch and headed out for a day on the water, the cook has the rest of the day to do the breakfast dishes, straighten up the cottage, conduct camp chores and prepare an evening meal for returning anglers. The next day a new cook is assigned and the process continues until everyone has had an opportunity to pull his or her weight around camp.

If money is a primary concern, camping at one of the many Canadian provincial parks is an excellent way to reduce costs. Like state or national parks in the U.S., provincial parks offer both rustic and modern campsite opportunities. A special fee permit is required to camp on crown land, of course.

This guide prepares a traditional shorelunch during a midday break. A hot shorelunch of walleye fillets is the highlight of many wilderness-fishing adventures.

Planning The Fly-In Trip

For many anglers fly-in trips are the essence of Canadian walleye fishing. It's hard to describe the excitement an angler feels when a float plane full of fishing gear and excited anglers lands on an uncharted wilderness lake. The anticipation and excitement can be overwhelming.

Fly-in trips provide the ultimate in wilderness-fishing adventures. Lakes accessible only by air receive the least amount of angling pressure and provide anglers the best opportunity for pristine walleye-fishing excitement.

Despite the glamour associated with fly-in fishing trips, not all these trips are luxury vacations. Some fly-in camps are extremely rustic, to say the least. Tent camps with dirt floors and the barest of essentials are common.

At the other extreme, fly-in fishing vacations costing upward of $2,000 per individual provide everything an angler could hope for in creature comforts, home-cooked meals and guided fishing adventures. Some lodges even have their own landing strips that accept propjets loaded with business executives. The average group of walleye fishermen falls somewhere in between. Although more expensive than drive-in trips, fly-in fishing vacations are well within the financial reach of most anglers.

How far north the anglers venture and the amount of creature comforts ultimately determine the final cost of fly-in trips. Anglers willing to accept rustic accommodations—tent camps or make-shift plywood cabins—can set up a fly-in fishing trip for less money than might be expected.

Most week-long, fly-in trips range from $500 to $1,000 per person. Airfare, boats, motors, boat fuel, cooking utensils and lodging are included in most packages. Food, bedding and transportation to and from the base camp are the angler's responsibility.

Avoiding The Pitfalls

When searching for a Canadian outfitter, check with a chamber of commerce in the region you plan to fish. Organizations such as the Northern Ontario Tourist Association will be happy to help anglers plan successful vacations.

References provided by the outfitter should be checked carefully. Even though no outfitter in his right mind would provide references from less-than-satisfied customers, anglers need to be aware of some common pitfalls associated with booking an outfitter, and ask the references specific questions. Many outfitters and lodge owners encourage new customers to book trips during time slots that are otherwise difficult to fill. The prime dates are reserved for their returning clientele. To avoid making a poorly timed trip, it's best to contact several lodges in the region you plan to visit and ask when walleye-fishing activity peaks.

June is the most popular period throughout southern to central Canada. Farther north, more consistent weather and fishing opportunities tend to be in July. Late summer and early fall can also provide excellent angling opportunities, as long as anglers realize that most fish will be deep at this time of year. It may take some specialized gear to catch them.

September, October and early November can bring bitter cold weather, but some of the finest trophy-class walleyes are taken once the leaves start to fall. Some anglers combine walleye fishing with moose, waterfowl or upland game hunting. If you can tolerate the cold, this season can be very exciting!

Where To Go

The list of walleye-fishing destinations across Canada is mind-boggling. Literally thousands of lakes harbor excellent populations of walleyes. Many lakes haven't had angling pressure from ice-out to the first snows of winter.

Rainy Lake
Located on the border of Minnesota and Ontario near International Falls, Rainy Lake is one of the most exciting fisheries in the wilderness. A beautiful summer-vacation destination, Rainy not only provides outstanding walleye-fishing opportunities, but crappies, northern pike, muskies and smallmouth bass abound in these waters, as well.

Walleyes are more easily found in late summer when the fish appear in large numbers on deep-water structure. Sunken islands and humps found in 20 to 40 feet of water are walleye magnets.

These deep-water fish can be taken with jigs; however, most anglers find slip-sinker rigs baited with leeches produce more fish. A bottom-bouncer sinker with a 48-inch snell and single hook also makes an excellent live-bait rigging option for deep-water walleyes. Bait the rig with a minnow, leech or 'crawler and slowly troll it back and forth across the humps.

One of the best ways to see and fish Rainy Lake is on a houseboat. Comfort plus mobility make houseboating a popular and productive way to fish this sprawling Canadian Shield lake.

Big Sand Lake
Located near Minaki, Ontario, Big Sand Lake, a classic shield lake, routinely coughs up limit-catches of walleyes. The fish in spring are located near the river mouths and gradually move deeper as the summer progresses. This body of water also has excellent trophy potential. In addition to walleyes, Big Sand cranks out excellent numbers of northern pike, smallmouth bass and muskies.

Pipestone Lake
Pipestone Lake, north of International Falls, Minnesota, contains a tremendous population of walleyes. Various fishing patterns produce walleyes on this body of water. Early in the spring, jigging and rigging near the river mouths provide consistent action. As summer progresses, the fish move into deep water and set up housekeeping on sunken reefs and islands in approximately 30 to 40 feet of water.

Rigging with jumbo leeches or pulling bottom bouncers armed

Large catches of small fish are common on many Canadian lakes. Eating-sized walleyes, like this stringer, abound in many waters.

with leeches or 'crawlers are the most effective ways to fool these deep-water fish.

Winnipeg River/Red River

The Winnipeg River near the community of Pine Falls is an outstanding walleye fishery. Lots of fish—and large fish—are common. Vertical jigging with a minnow is the best way to find quick action. The Red River just north of Winnipeg has similar potential. September and October are the best months to go.

Tobin Lake

Located in Nipawin, Saskatchewan, this walleye lake receives little fishing pressure. Because it's actually a reservoir, fish move from the dam site upstream to the main lake during spring and early summer.

Jig-and-minnow combinations work best in spring. During the summer, look for walleyes in deeper water where a slip rig or bottom bouncer and leech are excellent teasers.

Summing It Up

Walleye fishing in Canada has changed very little over the last 20 years. Although some fisheries have been damaged because of unchecked commercial and sport harvest, thousands of lakes still teem with walleyes just waiting to become shorelunches.

Imagining the beauty of the Canadian bush country is difficult. You need to see it for yourself. Despite slightly higher costs and, in some cases, inconveniences during border crossings, most U.S. anglers continue to find Canada irresistible.

=23=

Walleyes Beyond
The Heartland

Despite the fact that anglers spend more hours pursuing
walleyes in this country's heartland and Ontario than
in the rest of the country combined, there's no shortage of walleye-fishing opportunities outside this nucleus. Some of the finest and certainly the least-fished walleye waters are found south, east and west of what most anglers consider
walleye country. The Dakotas, Nebraska, Kansas, Wyoming and
Montana all offer Western walleye action that exceeds most Eastern standards.

In the South, Missouri, Oklahoma and Texas feature growing
walleye fisheries that see very little angling pressure. On the Eastern flank, Tennessee, Pennsylvania and New York also have
walleye-fishing paradises, yet you seldom hear anything about
these untapped fisheries.

There are many reasons why these fisheries have not received
the credit they deserve. For one thing, there are fewer anglers in
these areas who take advantage of the fishing opportunities or
spread the good word.

In the Dakotas, Nebraska, Kansas, Montana and Wyoming,
most of the cities aren't exactly bulging at the seams with people.
In agricultural and ranch lands the population often averages less
than 10 persons per square mile. (Compare that to a metropolitan
suburb and you'll quickly realize that most Western walleyes get
very little fishing pressure.)

Most anglers outside the heartland know little about walleyes

The impoundments of Wyoming, Montana and Colorado receive little fishing pressure by Eastern standards. Some waters feature a creel limit of 20 fish per day. A limit like that says it all!

Walleyes Beyond The Heartland   235

and how to catch them. When new fisheries develop, it often takes many years before local anglers learn when, where and how to catch the fish. On many waters, the fishing remains a mystery until a tournament comes to town.

Not so long ago, Michigan's Saginaw Bay was developing a reputation for being a walleye-fishing mecca. Despite the fact that walleyes weren't in short supply, local anglers had little success stringing together consistent catches.

Then came the area's first professional walleye tournament. At the time, most of the fish being caught were taken in the adjoining tributary streams. Biologists and anglers alike knew that Saginaw Bay held great walleye-fishing potential, but no one had been able to find and pattern significant numbers of fish. When the pros came to town all that changed.

Not being local anglers, these professional anglers began looking for fish in areas where the pros' experience told them the walleyes should be—not in areas where they wouldn't be. With their knowledge, equipment and experience, these walleye hounds soon ferreted out a good bite and set the stage for some serious Saginaw-Bay walleye catches.

The Saginaw Bay fishery was unleashed by a group of tournament pros who laid the ground work for further exploration. In the last few years, local and visiting anglers have transformed this appendage of Lake Huron into one of the best known and producing walleye fisheries in the nation.

New walleye fisheries and mysteries are uncovered every year by tournament anglers. The rapidly expanding range of the walleye proves that new, and perhaps even better, walleye fisheries are just around the corner.

Some of the best walleye waters in the nation are within a short drive of the walleye heartland. The Dakotas, Kansas and Nebraska are prime examples. Although these regions have been producing excellent walleye fishing since the early 1960s, few anglers besides the local residents have tapped into these bulging sportfishing opportunities.

North And South Dakota

Named after an Indian maiden, Lake Sakakawea in North Dakota is a great walleye fishery. A Missouri River reservoir, this fishery has gone through many changes in recent years. Drought and low-water levels have concentrated fish, impacted spawning success and threatened to bring this fishery to its knees.

Like all reservoirs, water levels in "Sak" affect sportfishing success. When water levels drop, fish become concentrated and more vulnerable to fishing pressure. Visiting anglers are encouraged to limit their harvest to smaller fish in order to prevent over-harvesting the adult spawning stock.

Summer and fall are the best times to visit Lake Sakakawea. The traditional, Missouri-River, bottom-bouncer sinker armed with a spinner and nightcrawler produces best in the summer. Local anglers prefer large (No. 4, 5 and 6), Colorado- and Indiana-style blades.

During fall, anglers do best dragging jigs and slip-sinker rigs tipped with large minnows. A red-tailed chub or sucker minnow has tempted many trophy walleyes from the depths of Lake Sakakawea. Located in South Dakota, Lake Oahe (pronounced Oh-wah'-hee) is actually a reservoir of the Missouri River. Fabled for producing trophy-class walleye, sauger and saugeye, Lake Oahe provides enormous walleye-sportfishing opportunities.

A huge body of water, Lake Oahe can be an intimidating fishery for first-time visitors. Over 230 miles long, this fishery features an astounding 2,250 miles of shoreline! Fortunately for visiting anglers, most fish are taken on jigs or spinner rigs fished near main lake points.

Keeping in mind that this sprawling reservoir has more points than an aroused porcupine, Lake Oahe is no pushover. Much of the best fishing centers in the dam end near the capital city of Pierre. A mecca for sportsmen, this growing Western city is the perfect starting point for anglers interested in fishing the main reservoir or Lake Sharpe (which begins below the Oahe dam).

Within the main reservoir, dozens of locations hold fish consistently. A few of the most popular spots include the Whitlock Recreation Area, Little Bend, Blue Blanket, Cow Creek and the waters around the mouths of the Cheyenne, Moreau and Grand Rivers.

Spring and fall are the best times to find pleasant weather and fishing conditions. Late fall provides the best opportunity for jumbo-walleye action. The mouth of the Cheyenne yields good catches of better-than-average-sized walleyes and an occasional trophy-class fish.

The Dakotas offer some great walleye-fishing potential to the avid angler. Sprawling reservoirs, such as Lake Oahe and Lake Sakakawea, are full of areas that have not been tapped by other anglers.

A jig tipped with a lively fathead or sucker minnow works best in spring and fall. Spring anglers stick with smaller minnows, while those who fish 4- to 6-inch sucker or chub minnows in the fall often collect the best catches.

The South Dakota summers usually are very hot and dry. Despite the heat, local anglers continue to catch excellent numbers of walleyes throughout July, August and September. Trolling bottom-bouncer sinkers armed with nightcrawler harnesses is the standard summer-fishing strategy.

Those anglers who plan to visit South Dakota in the summer should come prepared with plenty of sunscreen, protective light-colored clothing and a good fishing cap. Anglers should fish early and late in the day to avoid the suffocating heat.

Lake Sharpe is the reservoir created by Big Bend Dam some 80 miles downstream from Oahe Dam. With its upper end just below Oahe Dam, Lake Sharpe offers 200 miles of shoreline and a stable walleye population made up of fish averaging 2 to 3 pounds.

Below the dam at Pierre and throughout the lake, an excellent river fishery exists for walleyes and sauger. In spring and late fall, the fish are concentrated near the dam site. Throughout late spring and summer, walleyes can be found in the main lake in deeper water.

Complete Angler's Library

Anglers do well trolling minnow-style crankbaits along the riprap banks early in the spring and after the leaves fall in autumn. Night-fishing often produces the best action involving better-than-average-sized fish.

Jigs tipped with minnows are also excellent walleye/sauger producers throughout the year. The area directly beneath the dam at Pierre and near Antelope Creek is good during spring and fall.

During the summer, the stretch from West Bend to Joe Creek is a productive chunk of water. Jigs tipped with 'crawlers and spinner rigs are popular with local anglers.

Farther downstream, Lake Francis Case, which is sandwiched between Big Bend Dam and Fort Randall Dam at Pickstown, is approximately 107 miles long with over 540 miles of shoreline available to visiting anglers.

Some of the best fishing in Case and Sharpe occurs in the tailwater areas below the two dams. Fishing success begins as early as mid-February. During April and May, the Case reservoir heats up in the upper end near the town of Chamberlain. Limit catches of 1- to 3-pound fish are common in this area.

Although the fish often run smaller in Lake Francis Case than in other Missouri River impoundments, the numbers of fish taken compensate for the smaller size.

Jigs tipped with minnows, leeches or 'crawlers are the standard fare. Bonus catches include channel catfish and largemouth and smallmouth bass.

Kansas

The Glen Elder Reservoir in Kansas has been coming on strong for several years. Over 12,000 acres of prime walleye habitat make this fishery one of the largest and most productive walleye locations in the nation, especially in May and June.

Walleyes are often found suspended in flooded brush. Yo-yoing a jig amid this cover is an excellent way to tempt limit catches of 2- to 3-pound fish. Drift fishing the flats is also popular with locals; the Kansas wind always seems to cooperate. Anglers control their drifts by slowing boat speed with sea anchors. Electric or gas motors are used to steer the boat into productive waters.

Nebraska

Nebraska's Merritt Reservoir is currently the state's No. 1

walleye fishery. Located just south of the South Dakota border, Merritt is only 2,800 acres. Despite its small size, this impoundment produces a striking number of good-sized walleyes.

Angling tactics that work in other reservoir systems work equally well in Merritt. Jigs fished off main lake points and spinner rigs trolled over the flats produce most of the fish.

Lake McConoughy, a popular Platte-River impoundment, has had some ups and downs. The introduction of stripers temporarily brought on a decline of forage fish, damaging the walleye fishery. Recently, the lake has recovered and become a strong walleye fishery, although not at the level it once was. Spring and fall are the best times to fish, and slip-sinker rigging with oversized suckers or chubs is a difficult presentation to beat.

The Mountain States

Wyoming and Montana are becoming extremely exciting walleye-fishery states. Large reservoirs including Pathfinder, Seminoe and Fort Peck provide an enormous amount of prime walleye habitat. With light sportfishing pressure, it's not surprising that these reservoirs routinely provide large numbers of better-than-average-sized fish.

Pathfinder and Seminoe reservoirs, located in central Wyoming, are both part of the Platte River drainage basin. As with other reservoirs, the fishing is often a jig bite early in the year and a spinner bite later in the season. Jigs tipped with minnows are best on the points, and pulling worm harnesses along the flats produce best from June through August.

Both impoundments feature clear water. Night-fishing often produces the largest fish. Trophy-class walleyes are common, plus many 3- to 5-pound fish are taken. The daily creel limit on some waters is 20 fish!

Farther north, Fort Peck reservoir in Montana is the first major impoundment on the Missouri River. Known for producing huge sauger, this Western fishery teems with 2- to 4-pound sauger. Walleyes are also abundant in the reservoir; and hybrid-saugeyes are numerous, too.

Anglers are well-advised to concentrate on the main lake points. At times, the walleyes can be found in extremely shallow water. Casting or dragging jigs tipped with minnows or 'crawlers are the most popular angling methods.

Eastern Walleyes

Most Eastern walleye waters can't compete with the walleye populations in the heartland, throughout Ontario and, lately, in the Western states. However, these bodies of water show promise and provide anglers with a taste of walleye fishing in a region that offers a limited number of walleye fisheries.

Producing walleyes up to 12 pounds, Lake Chautauqua in New York State can be a difficult lake to fish during the warm-water periods. Heavy recreational boat traffic forces anglers to fish early and late in the day. The best fishing takes place in spring. Traditional jigging and rigging methods produce most of the fish.

In the northeastern corner of New York, the Thousand Islands region of Lake Ontario narrows down to where the St. Lawrence River flows toward the Atlantic Ocean. Fabled as a trophy-muskie region, walleyes and smallmouth bass also abound in this semi-wilderness area.

Similar in nature to northern Minnesota, the Thousand Islands area is a popular tourist destination. Walleyes are taken along the rocky shorelines and channel edges; narrows that provide stronger current seem to produce best.

Bay Of Quinte

This southern Ontario walleye hole is only a short drive from Toronto, Canada, yet few walleye anglers visit this quaint port city. Known primarily for its early-winter ice fishing, the Bay of Quinte yields an amazing number of trophy-sized walleyes to those anglers who can fish when the bite is best. First ice is the best time to snag a trophy-class fish. Depending upon the year, first ice could come before Christmas or as late as mid-January!

Jigging spoons tipped with minnows are the preferred lures, and anglers are well-advised to spool up with slightly heavier monofilament than normal. Big fish can easily break off 6- or 8-pound-test monofilament, especially when it's brittle from the cold. Most anglers depend upon 10- to 12-pound-test line to prevent unnecessary break-offs.

24

Trophy Walleyes
And The Future

Most serious walleye fishermen agree that a true brag-
ging-sized walleye tips the scales at 10 pounds or more.
Although the current world record is two and a half
times that size, few fish over the 10-pound mark are
taken from even the best fisheries.

The world-record, 25-pound walleye was taken in Old Hickory Lake near Nashville, Tennessee. Caught in 1960, the record
has stood for more than 30 years and seems to be in no serious
danger of tumbling.

Rarely have walleyes exceeding 20 pounds been taken. In fact,
anything that is more than 15 pounds is big news when it comes to
walleye fishing.

Although some reservoirs in the near South are capable of producing enormous walleyes, significant numbers of big fish aren't
in the cards. A lack of interest is a major reason these Southern
reservoirs don't yield more big walleyes.

Few Southern anglers have caught the walleye bug. Bass and
stripers are the most popular fish in this part of the world, and
walleye fishing just hasn't caught fire.

Greer's Ferry reservoir in Arkansas is a classic example. Considered one of the better trophy-walleye destinations, the new
world record may well reside in this central Arkansas impoundment. Unfortunately, the odds of traveling to Arkansas and coming home with a trophy aren't as good as you might expect.

Most of the trophy-walleye fishing activity is concentrated

Gary Parsons caught this 13-pound, 3-ounce lunker in northern Michigan's Little Bay de Noc. Known for yielding big fish, this body of water has coughed up 14- and 15-pound walleyes!

during the short spawning season. During the rest of the year, few walleyes are taken. A brief window of opportunity exists, but the likelihood of coming home with a brute walleye is probably better elsewhere.

Sorting Out The Best Big-Fish Waters

As mentioned, not every productive walleye hole has trophy-fish potential. A number of factors, including the size of the fishery, the available forage base, supplemental stocking programs, sport and commercial harvests and accessibility, influence the number of trophy-sized walleyes that any body of water is capable of offering.

The size of the fishery and its available forage base are two of the most important concerns. Large bodies of water, such as the Great Lakes, have the potential to produce enormous numbers of trophy-class walleyes. Fueled by an abundance of alewives, shad, smelt, emerald shiners, spottail shiners, johnny darters, yellow perch and other preferred forage fishes, walleyes grow quickly in these environments.

The length of time it takes a fish to reach the magic 10-pound barrier is considerably less in the forage-rich Great Lakes than other fisheries with a more restricted food supply. A fragile walleye

Trophy Walleyes And The Future   243 fingerling barely 3 inches long is transformed into a respectable wallhanger in six to eight short years. Less fertile waters often require 10 to 15 years to produce the same size fish.

The Great Lakes and a handful of other walleye factories can boast this type of trophy-fishing potential. The growth rates for walleyes in this region are among the fastest in the country.

Supplemental stocking programs in many waters also increase the chances that large numbers of fish live long enough to achieve trophy status. The Great Lakes and many connecting tributaries currently offer some of the best trophy walleye fishing potential available anywhere in North America.

A comprehensive trophy hunt is a lifetime pursuit. Like a white-tailed buck with a beaming rack, trophy walleyes are tough to come by. Those anglers willing to travel the extra distance and fish the extra hours have the odds of landing a true trophy. The rest is mostly luck.

Managing The Resource

Unlike many other species of fish, the mystique involving walleye fishing is just beginning to unfold. Interest in catching this species has never been higher, and research concerning the management of walleyes as a sportfishing resource hasn't even come close to peaking.

Despite all we've learned in the past few years, there is much more we don't understand. As the search for more and better ways to catch walleyes continues, anglers should acknowledge sportfisheries as precious resources.

Often taken for granted, walleyes are a renewable resource that when managed properly provide the ideal balance of sport and tablefare qualities. Few fish have as much to offer the sporting public as walleyes, sauger and saugeye.

Conscientious management is without a doubt the key to maintaining our rich sportfisheries. Many states and provinces have specialized fishing regulations, protecting the primary spawning stock while allowing a reasonable harvest of smaller fish.

The concept of selective harvest is something all anglers must consider and accept in order to continue the growth and expansion of fisheries. Each year the number of anglers increases. Keeping up with the demand for quality sportfishing is a burden all fishermen—not just fisheries managers—must shoulder.

If sportfishing stocks are to remain abundant, anglers must play an active role in resource management. This angler is releasing an eating-sized walleye. Although the law allows him five fish, this angler decided to take home only three. He is practicing a form of selective harvesting.

The Future Of Walleye Fishing

The future of walleye fishing across the North American continent is promising indeed. The heartland of walleye fishing continues to hold its own despite intense fishing pressure. The Great Lakes have been yielding walleyes like never before, and the far West looms as the next big walleye mecca.

The development of this species in the mountain states has been very successful. Throughout Colorado, Wyoming and Montana, many reservoirs are providing almost unlimited walleye-fishing opportunities.

The fish populations are on a steady rise, yet angling pressure is sparse by Eastern standards. Not only are walleyes plentiful, but the average size taken by sportfishermen in the Western states is nearly twice as large as the classic heartland fisheries. Naturally, trophy-sized fish are also in good supply.

The Great Lakes are no less impressive than the Western reservoirs. Planted fisheries in Saginaw Bay, Sturgeon Bay, Little Bay de Noc, and Lake Huron are yielding record sportfishing catches. Lake Erie, Lake St. Clair, the Bay of Quinte, Lake Ontario and the Detroit and St. Clair Rivers all contribute enormous schools of naturally reared fish to the largest walleye-fishing melting pot in the world.

Unfortunately, none of these fisheries is free from problems threatening the very existence of sportfishing in this country. Commercial fishing conducted by native Americans and corporate businesses continues to threaten sportfisheries across North America. Millions of pounds of walleyes are harvested every year for the commercial market place. Many are taken during the spawn when adult fish are concentrated in small areas.

In some areas, it isn't the walleyes but the food they eat that's threatened. The harvest of alewives, chubs, smelt and other forage fish for human and feline consumption poses an ominous cloud of doubt over many Great Lakes fisheries. No one knows for sure how long the stocks of forage fish will last.

Sportfishing Trends

On a brighter note, the way anglers catch walleyes has developed into some interesting patterns. For many years, jigging and rigging were considered the only serious ways to fish for walleyes. All that has changed with the advent of the Great Lakes and Western reservoir walleye boom.

Jigging and live-bait rigging will always be important, but more anglers are discovering that trolling crankbaits and various forms of live-bait rigs is productive and exciting. Planer boards, downriggers, diving planes, lead-core line and wire line are becoming familiar sights on many walleye boats. Spoons, plugs and nightcrawler harnesses make up the list of the hottest walleye-fishing lures.

The advent of tournament fishing has also made many contributions to walleye fishing. Few things motivate people more than the pursuit of fame and fortune. Tournament anglers pound the waters to develop new and better fishing presentations. Better quality fishing equipment, improved marine products and a better understanding of the role anglers play in the sportfishing scene are all benefits brought about by tournaments.

Evolution of catch-and-release ethics, selective harvest regulations, improved live-release methods, conservation fees paid by tournament anglers and other positive elements of sportfishing can be directly linked to tournament fishing.

Index